Room

Within

The Heart

Sherron Minerva Thomas

Olympus Story House

TABLE OF CONTENTS

Introduction

The word "heart" has come to mean many things. It primarily refers to the muscular organ with four chambers located on the left side of the chest, which is responsible for pumping blood around the body. Figuratively, it can refer to the center of something. For example, someone may speak of the "heart of the matter", i.e., the most important aspect of something. This usage is analogous to the important role the heart plays in the human body. Additionally, the meaning of the word "heart" varies according to the field of study in which it is used. In biology and the medical sciences, the word simply refers to the anatomic heart – the organ that pumps blood. In psychology, it refers to the mind as the center of thought and personality. Socially, the word refers to the center of emotion and feeling. It is at this level that a person can love someone with all their "heart." There is a long-standing debate about whether people think and feel with their hearts, brains, or a combination of the two. According to Rollin McCarthy, "it is shown that the heart is a key component of the emotional system, thus providing a physiological basis for the long-acknowledged link between the heart and our emotional life." This book examines this debate in the context of behavior modification. It looks at the ways through which the heart expresses itself and how its expression may be affected by an individual's internal and external environments. This book aims to address the following: What are the access points to the mind? How much room truly exists in the heart? Is there actually a relationship between what humans accept into their minds and the moral quality of their lives? If this is so, how many people are getting what they want from their hearts by making conscious choices about what they allow into their hearts in the first place?

This book is divided into ten chapters. Chapter one examines the age-old debate about the actual location of the mind. Is the human mind a physical organ located in the heart or the brain? Is it a psychological creation that encompasses the two organs? The concept of the mind is often used interchangeably with the concept of the heart. Chapter two attempts to evaluate the actual capacity of the heart or mind. How much can the heart really take? What kind of content fills the heart? How does the heart feel? Do emotions influence human behavior? How do emotions accomplish this? Chapter three focuses on the access routes to the heart. If there is room in the heart and can indeed be filled with content, then how does this content enter the heart? Are there entry points into the heart? If there are, how do the various kinds of content impact the heart? Where this impact is not desired, can people utilize certain methods to stem intrusion into these routes? This chapter also focuses on safeguarding the heart. How can we be protective of our hearts and keep our minds clean? The goal of this book is to equip its readers with knowledge of how the human mind functions in collaboration with the heart because what we think we also feel and what affects the heart affects how we think. Millions of people around the world are held captive by addictions from which they desire freedom. However, this freedom has been difficult (if not impossible) to achieve due to a lack of understanding of the thought processes they permit in their hearts. Societies are fearful of the predictable and, apparently, unstoppable descent into the valley of self-destruction orchestrated by various agents who have constantly bombarded the hearts and minds of their young ones. If societies are to halt the progress of this undesirable outcome, they must be more cautious about the content they allow to influence the hearts and minds of their young ones. If societies can do this, is it possible that we will see the beginnings of societal restorations? Of course, making the necessary changes will not be easy, but is the outcome not worth the effort?

I began writing this book many years ago, as many as 21 years while I was attending the Inter-American University of Puerto Rico Metropolitan Campus. One morning as I walked down the hill from my apartment for the two-mile journey to the college, my heart was full of a myriad of emotions, especially that I had to walk past a dangerous area. The heaviness in my heart's brain transferred to my mind's brain and vice versa as my thoughts began writing "room within", the conscience of humanity and how we are to each other. Some of these thoughts stemmed from incidents I experienced while within those environments. I lived up a hillside, two miles from the college. The bustle of a supermarket and small bar stood just outside the University. When I walked to school, I had to pass the projects daily, sometimes at night when the bus hours stopped until I made friends who did not mind taking me home. Along the way, I'd see people fighting and cursing at each other, and the atmosphere was pungent. Many nights gun shots riddled the air and my first time experiencing the country's election results, I observed the air exuded a combination of firecrackers and gunshots of all calibers intertwined between the communities. I eventually moved to another area I thought would be safer in Guaynabo just a few blocks below a Police Station and the church I attended. One evening, the celebrations got out of hand and the air was practically black with the smell of these powders fused. This time my mom and I were relaxing out on the second-floor apartment balcony and we both jumped up almost instantaneously and bolted to the inside door. Although vibrantly aged, my mom had fast feet. The room within my heart held so many different emotions that the expressions and controversies demonstrated were astonishing, to say the least, and for me, uncomfortable because what goes up must come down. Passing through Calle De Diego, an area known to debut violence, to my dentist to care for my braces was a monthly feat. We never know who is within our environment, but we can always trust in God. A scripture from the Book of Wisdom quickly came to mind and still does, "Trust in the LORD with all your heart and lean not on your own understanding; in all your ways submit to him, and he will make your paths straight. (Proverbs 3:5-6)". This scripture helps bring a sense of peace amid the chaotic world and vibrant confidence that a supreme Almighty God is our strength and guide.

Nineteen of those twenty-one years since I conceived to write this book, I spent in the US Army; and my experiences carved many writings on my heart that I am so glad I did not publish before. I realized the need to define the room within 'what' and this enabled the growth of "Room Within The Heart." My own heart has a myriad of experiences that collaboratively infused a kaleidoscope of my genuine thoughts and feelings. For the past recent years, I awoke many nights to the drum of my heart racing. It beats extremely fast, and I can feel my entire body, my fingers, and toes begin a tense rhythmic pulse. It seems like everywhere that has a pulse is beating extremely fast. I touch my heart and surely, it's pushing against my palm like it wants freedom from my body. My breathing is completely thrown off; it's erratic and laborious. My body feels heavy as though laden from working hard but it's at 3 am sometimes it comes on at any wee morning hours. It's a very scary feeling, a panic attack that comes on as my heart races to replenish oxygen that plummets while I'm asleep and unaware. I must sit up, consciously take deep breaths, and tell my mind, "It's ok just relax", and I recall soothing scriptures, mainly, "Be strong and take heart, all you who hope in the Lord," Ps 31:23. I find a calm space after hours of pacing each breath while hot tears stream and caress each cheek.

The frequency of these episodes is more often and because they occur while I'm asleep, I cannot seem to prevent these occurrences. I call on the only being, my Savior who is present and is in control, a fusion of teary prayerful praise because that is all I can do. Our heart is diverse in what it feels in the natural and how it is referred to metaphorically. I share the writings in my heart; as Luke so eloquently stated "out of the abundance of the heart, the mouth speaks in chapter 6 verse 45", although many times, I protect my thoughts within.

Some may think I'm the least likely to have written this book, I may not be a doctor, frankly far from it and I'm not a counselor but I have a heart that cares for everyone regardless of who they claim to be, a heart that desires, a heart that thinks and understands, and a heart that loves wholesomely. This intro may seem like I had a tough knock life, but not in the least. I have a life that is groomed with the presence of God who continues to guide the core of my heart, the room where *He Lives*.

CHAPTER ONE

HEART VERSUS BRAIN: WHERE IS THE CONNECTION?

An article by Dr. John P. Glynn of the Tibb Institute (2012) captures the heart versus mind debate quite succinctly. In the article, Dr. Glynn observes that the word "heart" conjures positive images of emotions such as love, kindness, gratitude, and sincerity. For some, it may also suggest negative thoughts like grief, loneliness, misery, and fear. The word has long been embedded in our everyday language and is widely used in many expressions such as "heart-warming", "heart sore", "heart-to-heart", etc. In contrast, although indispensable to life, organs like the kidneys, liver, or lungs do not live off much in terms of metaphors that describe powerful emotions and qualities. Traditionally, the heart is the emblem of emotions, courage, and humanity. In the time of Hippocrates and other pioneers, the heart was seen as one of three major organs (the brain and the liver were the other two). This trio of major organs controlled every aspect of the body's physical and mental activity. Although the role of the heart in pumping blood through the body was recognized and accepted, the actual details of the mechanisms involved were not to be identified until well into the future. In addition, the Vital Faculty (seated in the heart), was thought to be responsible for not only our emotional states but also for the various mechanisms through which we engage with the outside world.

Discoveries made in the seventeenth century revealed the precise workings of the circulatory system. This led to the displacement of ideas concerning the heart's central role, which was unceremoniously relegated to a mere blood pump - admittedly, a very sophisticated one. Its relation to the emotions was discounted in favor of the activities of the brain. However, worse was to come: the brain was deemed the master of the body, the heart but one of its servants. The brain commands, the heart obeys and responds, immediately changing the rhythm, rate, or force of contraction.

Recently, there has been a revival of interest in the working of the heart, ushered in by the arrival of new technology and attendant discoveries. For example, we now know that there is a dynamic and continuous two-way exchange of information between the heart and the brain. We also know that the heart is no mere blood pump but has other functions that were only recently discovered. One such discovery demonstrated that the heart is self-regulating in that it acts as an endocrine gland: it secretes several hormones (adrenaline, for example) that can influence blood flow. The heart also secretes the hormone oxytocin, previously thought to be confined to the brain alone. This hormone, beloved of mothers-to-be, is responsible for uterine contractions in childbirth and lactation. Interestingly, this same hormone (dubbed the "love hormone") is central to the development of trust, empathy, and pair-bonding, as well as certain emotions like anxiety, envy, and calmness.

Many researchers now think that the heart has its own "built-in brain". Studies show that the heart is capable of crunching masses of data arising from all parts of the body and transmitting this information to the central nervous system via different pathways. It also possesses memory. There is also the intriguing and bizarre observation that, when a heart is surgically transplanted, emotions and behaviors typical of the donor are picked up by the recipient. For example, a teetotaler recipient took to drinking beer after receiving a heart from an alcoholic donor. In contrast, other transplants involving kidneys, lungs, pancreas, or other organs do not seem to produce this strange phenomenon.

How relevant is this information to our overall health? Well, the heart is, arguably, the part of the body that influences our quality of life, so the findings cited above are quite relevant. We know that positive emotions like joy, empathy, and love help create harmony in the heart and contribute to a happier, healthier and even longer life. The opposite is true of negative emotions like uncontrolled anger, constant worry, and crippling depression. The Tibb Institute has long accepted that a person's emotional state significantly influences one's emotional state is listed amongst the major Lifestyle Factors, alongside food, breathing, sleep, exercise, and toxin elimination. On the one hand, a sound emotional state is regarded as an important aspect of personal wellness. Such is why active measures that limit the effects of negative emotions on a person's health are part of the therapies offered today. On the other hand, there is now a wealth of clinical evidence that connects the heart to emotional turmoil. For instance, the risk of heart disease rises strikingly in people who experience frequent episodes of anger or worry. In addition, highly anxious men are up to six times more likely to suffer sudden cardiac arrest. Interestingly, the risk posed by emotional stress in the form of heart disease and cancer is greater than the risks posed by smoking, high blood pressure, and high cholesterol levels. Also, people who are in control of their emotional states are more likely to live within a given period than those who are not coping well with said states. We also know that sincere, positive feelings boost the immune system, while negative emotions often have the opposite effect. This explains why people who are in thrall to negative emotions are much more prone to developing illnesses and chronic diseases.

Robinson and Fetterman (2013) also weighed in on the discussion about the heart and brain. They observe that the "Two body parts – the head and the heart – have been ascribed particular psychological significance throughout the history of Western civilization." They cite Plato (trans. 1987) to be among the first to suggest that the head is the source of rational wisdom, whereas the heart is the source of the passions. Philosophers and writers after Plato elaborated on the purported significance of the head versus the heart. They spoke of rational thinking, emotional responses, and decision making, all in a way that preserves Plato's presumed functions of these two organs.

Robinson and Fetterman further observe that, in our daily lives, we frequently make references to the head or the heart. To "use one's head" means to think rationally and logically about a problem, whereas to "lose one's head" means to lose the capacity for clear thinking. The organ located in the head – the brain – is also used to characterize intelligence (e.g., "he has a brain", "she is brainy", and so on). On the other hand, to be "stuck in one's head" suggests a lack of social reflected in our stereotyping of "brainy" individuals as being more interested in intellectual pursuits than in people. Thus, common metaphors for the head suggest greater rationality and intelligence, albeit being indicative of some lack of social connection.

Like brain metaphors, heart metaphors can also be two-fold. For example, to "follow one's heart" means to let one's emotions dictate one's life choices. On the other hand, those who dwell on adverse personal events can be prone to "heartache". There is also a different class of metaphors that link the heart to greater social connection and caring. For example, a person "has a heart" to the extent that they care about others. Such caring individuals are also characterized as "having a big heart" or "warm heart". In sum, metaphors for the heart suggest a capacity for both emotions and their expression.

HeartMath (2002) reports that the brain and the heart are not alienated from each other. There is a nervous system pathway that carries signals from the heart to the brain, just as there is one that carries messages from the brain to the heart. Surprisingly, the heart sends more signals to the brain than the brain sends to the heart! In a way, we could say that the heart and brain "talk" to one another; together, they "talk" to the body. The signals they send, whether harmonious or chaotic, can deeply impact how we feel and act. Nerve impulses from the heart are received first at the first brain level, then move into the brain's higher centers (second and third levels), affecting how we feel, think, perceive, and perform. Jagged and irregular heart rhythms send a message to the brain that we are upset. On the other hand, smooth, harmonious heart rhythms send a signal to the brain, letting it know that everything is alright.

According to Linden (2014), "Even the ancient Greeks knew that body and mind were interlinked, that one influenced the other. On the other hand, the contemporary practice of medicine has seen a major shift toward specialty care, focusing more on individual organs than on the whole patient. However, today's family physicians tell us that over half their patients who present with physical symptoms have underlying stress and emotional problems that need treating more than these physical symptoms do. Even common sense tells you that a patient with insomnia who also reports marital problems and a fear of losing his job shouldn't receive just medication for his sleep problems as a primary treatment. Because the mind-body linkages flow both ways, asking questions about causality is tricky.

On the other hand, for example, depression has a role in the causes of heart disease. In diagnosed cardiac patients, depression is known to increase mortality. This is at least partly explained by the fact that depressed patients are less likely to follow a diet or exercise or take their medications." From this excerpt, we should note two things: 1) it is obvious that there are some words that are usually mentioned once a conversation about the heart is started. Such words include "mind" and "emotion" 2) it is also clear that the dividing line between the anatomical body and the psychological mind is a thin one, leading Dr. Linden to talk of "mind-body linkages", a compound word that encompasses both.

The Royal Institute of Philosophy generally classifies the problems of the philosophy of mind into two categories. The first is a category of epistemological questions that are concerned with what is knowable when it comes to the mind. These include questions about how we can know the mental states of others and ourselves and the nature of these forms of knowledge. The second category consists of metaphysical questions concerned with the fundamental structure of the mind. For the last three centuries or so, the problem that has dominated the philosophy of mind has been a metaphysical one: the mind-body problem.

On the face of it, the mind-body problem seems to be a relatively simple one. It amounts to the saying that there is a relationship between our minds (or mental states) and our bodies (or brains). Why should this be a problem at all? The problem arises from two sets of intuitions, both of which seem quite compelling.

The first of these is the intuition that the mind and body are two distinctly different kinds of things. The body is an extended object in the physical world – it has a size, a weight, a shape, and a spatiotemporal location; I can feel it, taste it, hear it, smell it, and see it. Like other physical objects, the body can interact with the things around it. For example, my body gets onto trains, sits on chairs, picks up coffee mugs, and shakes hands with other bodies. Moreover, all of this is done in a way that would seem perfectly reasonable to a physicist. Just like other objects in the world, our bodies conform to natural and physical laws – the laws of gravity, causation, motion, and so on. In short, our bodies seem to be just like other physical things. The same can be said of our brains. In contrast, the mind does not seem to be like this at all. Our mental states are not things we can locate in the physical world or encounter through the senses; therefore, we must be wary of taking things in this direction. For example, if we start asking whether our mental states are subject to the laws of gravity or if they can get on trains or if they weigh more than a bag of sugar, we will end up with things not making much sense. At best, the things that we can ascribe to mental states are things like consciousness, intentionality, subjectivity, comparison to experiences or sensations, etc. These are features that seem to have no place in our purely physical descriptions of our bodies.

Initial considerations might lead us to view our bodies and minds as two vastly different kinds of entities. However, it is plain to anyone who has ever had both a mind and a body that they are more deeply bound up than this intuition of distinction might lead us to believe. My body is not just a vehicle for my mental life. Every thought I think, every action I perform, and everything I experience involves a complex and indissoluble engagement of mind and body. As René Descartes (the founder of the contemporary philosophy of mind) famously argued: "I am not only lodged in my body as a pilot in a vessel, but that I am besides so intimately conjoined, and as it was intermixed with it, that my mind and body compose a certain unity."

If we take the intuitions of the last two paragraphs too seriously, we are in danger of slipping into just this kind of picture of the mind-body relation. What, then, is the right way to understand the metaphysical relationship between my mind and my body that will accommodate both the intuition of distinctness and the thought that our minds and bodies are deeply interconnected?

The institute outlines several views that exist on the mind-body phenomenon. They are theories that have been developed to explain the relationship that exists between the mind and the body. The first theory, substance dualism, says that the mind and the body are distinctly different. The body is made of a physical substance, while the mind, being of a ghostly nature, is made of a non-physical mental substance. The second theory is called reductive materialism. According to reductive materialists, there is only one kind of substance in the world: the physical kind. When we talk about mental states and events, we are really talking about physical states, even if we do not always realize it. A third theory is a kind of compromise between the first two. Supporters of non-reductive materialism agree with reductive materialists in their assertion that only physical substances exist in the world. However, they disagree with the reductive materialists when the latter claim that physical stuff is all there is to mental phenomena. Even if our mental states and events depend on our physical states, facts concerning our mental lives cannot be reduced to facts concerning our physical makeup. A fourth response to the mind-body problem is called eliminative materialism. Like the other two kinds of materialists, eliminative materialists only believe in physical substances. Eliminative materialists, however, are far more radical than other kinds of materialists because they claim that mental phenomena are not only dependent on, or are reducible to, the physical domain — they claim that mental phenomena do not even exist!

According to the Reschini Group (2007), "Even though the brain and the heart are located far from one another in the body, they are intrinsically connected and have a significant impact on how each other functions. The two organs communicate via the muscular walls around the heart, which are connected to the brain in the circulatory system. As the brain releases hormones telling the body what to do, receptor cells in your blood vessels pick up these messages. In addition, there are nerve endings that travel from the brain to the heart's muscular walls. These nerves send messages to the muscle tissue to either relax or contract. Since these two organs communicate, mental health can dramatically affect heart health and vice versa." This demonstrates that, together, the anatomical heart and the human brain create the mind. Salem (2007) also admits that the concept of mind is of central importance to psychiatrists and psychologists. However, in most formal textbooks, little attention has been given to this important issue, which is usually studied under the section of 'Philosophical aspects of psychiatry/psychology'. In any case, the practicing psychiatrist should have a working model of the mind so that he may better understand his patient's problems (Salem, 2004).

In many cultures throughout history, the heart has been considered the source of emotions, passion, and wisdom. People were also said to experience the feeling or sensation of love and other emotional states in the area that coincides with the heart. There are stories of how individuals with heart surgeries heal differently when they take on positive mental aspirations. I watched the phenomenon of two individuals finding love amid recovery and how their hearts took on a different rhythm and began healing faster. This phenomenon puzzled the doctors. The underlying factor is "LOVE," which heals us from the inside. Interestingly, recent studies have explored physiological mechanisms by which the heart communicates with the brain, thereby influencing information processing, perceptions, emotions, and health. These studies explain how and why the heart affects mental clarity, creativity, and emotional balance.

It has long been known that changes in emotions are accompanied by predictable changes in heart rate, blood pressure, respiration, and digestion. Also, when we are excited, the sympathetic division of the autonomic nervous system energizes us for fight or flight. At other, more quiet times, the parasympathetic component cools us down. This perspective assumes that the autonomic nervous system and the physiological responses move in concert with the brain's response to given stimuli (Rein, Atkinson, et al. 1995). Recent research has found that the heart communicates with the brain in ways that significantly affect how we perceive and react to the world. Researchers found that the heart seemed to have its own peculiar logic, which frequently diverged from the direction of the autonomic nervous system. For example, it was observed that the heart appeared to be sending meaningful messages to the brain, which the brain understood and acted on (Lacey and Lacey, 1978). Moreover, neurophysiologists discovered a neural pathway and mechanism whereby input from the heart to the brain could inhibit or facilitate the brain's electrical activity (McCraty, 2002).

After extensive research, Armour (1994) introduced the concept

8

of the functional 'heart brain'. His work revealed that the heart has a complex nervous system that is sophisticated enough to qualify as a 'little brain' in its own right. The heart's brain is an intricate network of several types of neurons, neurotransmitters, proteins, and support cells similar to those found in the brain proper. Its elaborate circuitry enables it to act independently of the cranial brain – to learn, remember, and even feel and sense. The heart's nervous system contains around 40,000 neurons called sensory neurites (Armour, 1991).

Information from the heart — including sensations — is sent to the brain through several afferents. These afferent nerve pathways enter the brain at the area of the medulla and cascade up into the higher centers of the brain, where they can influence perception, decision-making, and other cognitive processes (Armour, 2004). The study revealed that the heart operates and processes information independently of the brain or nervous system. This is what allows a heart transplant to work. Normally, the heart communicates with the brain via nerve fibers running through the vagus nerve and the spinal column. In a transplanted heart, these nerve connections do not reconnect for an extended period. Nevertheless, the heart is able to function in its new host because of its intrinsic nervous system (Murphy, et al. 2000). Research has also demonstrated that the heart communicates information to the brain and the body via electromagnetic field interactions. The heart generates the body's most powerful and most extensive rhythmic electromagnetic field. The heart's magnetic component is about 500 times stronger than the brain's magnetic field and can be detected several feet away from the body. It was proposed that this heart field acts as a carrier wave for information which provides a synchronizing signal for the entire body (McCraty, Bradley & Tomasino, 2004). There is no evidence for a subtle yet influential electromagnetic or 'energetic' communication system that operates just below our conscious awareness. Energetic interactions possibly contribute to the 'magnetic' attractions or repulsions that occur between individuals. It was also found that a person's brain waves can synchronize with another person's heart (McCraty, 2004).

Another component of the heart-brain communication system

was provided by researchers studying the hormonal system. In 1983, the heart was reclassified as an endocrine gland when an atrial natriuretic factor (ANF) produced and released by the heart was isolated. This hormone exerts an effect on the blood vessels, the kidneys, the adrenal glands, and several regulatory regions of the brain. It was also found that the heart contains a cell type known as 'intrinsic cardiac adrenergic' (ICA) cells. These cells release noradrenaline and dopamine neurotransmitters once thought to be produced only by neurons in the CNS. More recently, it was discovered that the heart also secretes oxytocin, which is commonly referred to as the 'love' or bonding hormone. In addition to its functions in childbirth and lactation, recent evidence indicates that this hormone is also involved in cognition, tolerance, adaptation, complex sexual and maternal behaviors, learning social cues, and the establishment of enduring pair bonds.

Data indicates that when heart rhythm patterns are coherent, the neural information sent to the brain facilitates cortical function. This effect is often experienced as heightened mental clarity, improved decision-making, and increased creativity. Additionally, coherent input from the heart tends to facilitate the experience of positive feelings. This may explain why most people associate love and other positive feelings with the heart and why many people feel or sense these emotions in the area that coincides with the heart.

Research has shown that the heart's afferent neurological signals directly affect activity in the amygdala (an important emotional processing center in the brain) and associated nuclei. The amygdala is a key brain center that coordinates behavioral, immunological, and neuroendocrine responses to environmental threats. It compares incoming emotional signals with stored emotional memories and accordingly makes instantaneous decisions about the level of perceived threat. Due to its extensive connections to the limbic system, it is able to take over the neural pathways, activating the autonomic nervous system and emotional response before the higher brain centers receive the sensory information (Rein, McCraty and Atkinson, 1995 & McCraty et al. 1995).

A very interesting research has shown that the heart is involved in the processing and decoding of intuitive information (McCraty, Atkinson & Bradley, 2004). Previous data suggest that the heart's field was directly involved in intuitive perception, through its coupling with an energetic information field outside the bounds of space and time (Childre & McCraty, 2001). Using a rigorous experimental design, there was evidence that both the heart and brain receive and respond to information about a future event before the event actually happens. The heart, even more surprisingly, appears to receive this intuitive information before the brain (McCraty, Atkinson & Bradley, 2004).

McCraty also observes the raging debate over the origin of emotions and the difference between emotions and intellect. He believes that the relationship between the mind and emotions has been deliberated throughout history, with most schools of thought drawing a boundary between them. Perception, appraisal, arousal, attention, memory, thinking, reasoning, and problem-solving are often grouped together under the broader heading of cognition or the mental system. On the other hand, the emotional system encompasses feelings, which can span a range of intensity. The importance of gaining a deeper understanding of the emotional system has become increasingly recognized as an important scientific undertaking, as it has become clear that emotions underlie the majority of the stress we experience, influence our decisions, provide the motivation for our actions, and create the textures that determine our quality of life. In recent years, the concept of "emotional intelligence" has emerged, claiming that emotional maturity is as important as our mental abilities in personal and professional spheres. Emotional competency often outweighs the cognitive in determining success.

The tendency to view emotions as operating separately and apart from rational or intellectual capacities dates back to the times of the ancient Greeks. Thus, historically, thinking and feeling—or intellect and emotion—have often been portrayed as opposing forces engaged in an incessant battle for control over the human psyche. Plato maintained that strong emotions made it impossible for him to think and described emotions as wild horses that had to be reined in by the intellect, while Christian theology has traditionally regarded many emotions as sins and temptations to be overcome by reason and willpower. Traditionally, the intellect was held in high regard, while emotions were considered "irrational" and received little recognition. However, a modern-day examination of emotions presents us with an entirely new perspective, providing a more comprehensive understanding of the emotional system and illuminating the critical roles that emotions play in human experience, performance, and rationality.

From the foregoing discussion, one can conclude that mankind has always been interested in the connection between the brain and the heart. He has instinctively believed the heart to be the seat of emotion and the brain to be the seat of the intellect. These two, interacting closely, produce the concept of the mind, which is not an anatomical organ. In general conversation, the heart and the mind are often used interchangeably to represent either emotion or intellect. It does not seem to matter very much in daily conversations that there are differences between the two. In the next chapter, we are going to look at how the heart feels and how emotions influence human behavior.

CHAPTER TWO

HOW MUCH ROOM EXISTS IN THE MIND?

W e established in chapter one that the debate over the actual location of the mind is traceable to ancient times. It is also clear that neither the brain nor the heart can claim monopoly hosting rights to the mind. The mind is a function of the two organs and much more. In this chapter, we are going to look at the capacity of the mind. What is the composition or function of the mind? Is the mind affected by its content? How is this possible?

Emotions: How Does The Heart Feel?

According to HeartMath (2002), the word "emotion" can be defined as "energy in motion." An emotion is a strong feeling—a feeling such as joy, sorrow, or anger—that moves us. The experience of emotion makes life matter. It transforms our world from a series of events and facts into a living, breathing experience. For instance, you have had a rotten day, you come home, and your dog is wildly wagging his whole body because he loves you no matter what. Just seeing him, you start to ease up and forget about your awful day. You may not always be aware of your deeper feelings and how these feelings are affecting your body, energy, thoughts, and relationships. You might notice tension or an upset stomach. Sometimes, you might even feel your heart pounding in your chest.

In fact, one of the easiest ways that scientists observe how feelings affect our bodies is in the effects they have on our heart rhythms. When emotions are strong, they can be detected in the changing pattern of our heart rhythms. When people are frustrated, scared, worried, angry, or upset, their heart rhythms are uneven and irregular. When these uneven, irregular heart rhythms are viewed on a computer screen, they look like jagged mountain peaks. When we are upset, it's usually hard to think clearly. Making a wise choice is tough for anyone when they are emotionally upset. Have you ever said something to a friend in a moment of anger that you later regretted?

However, when we feel confident and secure, feel cared for, or appreciate someone or something, our heart rhythms are smooth. Scientists now know that the heart and brain are connected, and that smooth and even heart rhythms make it easier to think clearly and make better decisions. Although the feeling is traditionally talked about as something coming from the heart, we have established that the brain, in fact, plays a bigger role in our emotions. The brain is divided into three levels, each of which has a particular function in the overall emotional state of an individual. The first brain controls your instincts, reflexes, and basic physical functioning. Amphibians (for example, frogs and salamanders), reptiles (such as alligators, lizards, and snakes), and birds of all kinds have only this part of the brain. They act and behave mainly from their instincts. The first brain cannot solve math problems, but without it, we could not survive. Our instinctual awareness of danger comes from this brain level. When we are hungry or thirsty, the survival instincts of the first brain will let us know and cause us to eat or drink. If this were the only brain level we had, we would rush to the food, pick it up, and gulp it down instead of standing in a lunch line when we are hungry.

The second brain is involved in many of our feelings and emotions. Without this brain, we would not have feelings of sadness or joy. Feelings of anger, fear, territoriality (protecting our turf), as well as feelings of security, pleasure, and the joy of bonding with others, are all possible because of the second brain. Many animals, such as dogs and cats, have this brain level as well. This part of the brain gives us the memory of past events. When you and a friend see each other, memories of your last conversation and how you feel about each other are available to you because of the structures and circuits in the second brain that store those memories. The second brain also allows for us to have hindsight. This means that we can learn from our past mistakes and successes.

The third brain, sometimes called the cortex, is involved in thinking, problem-solving, goal-setting, and planning. This part of the brain provides you with foresight, an important ability that allows you to see ahead and consider the consequences of your decisions before acting on them. This is an advantage over the second brain, where unmanaged emotions can push you to act without considering future results. The third brain also monitors the second brain's activity and allows you to name and sort out your feelings and emotions. It can then help you decide what the best course of action may be for any situation. For example, a comment from a classmate offends you, and you feel hurt or angry. You have to decide how you will respond. The third brain reviews several possibilities: seek revenge, try to talk and resolve the conflict, and let it go, forgive, or consider other options. It is the ability to understand the situation from many angles that can lead to a more intelligent decision. The third brain can also help you notice when you are acting against what you feel is right. Some call this being aware of your conscience.

While all three brain levels interact all the time, all three need to work together in harmony should you want to use all of the abilities you have. In other words, they have to be in sync with one another. However, this is not always the case. Often, we rely too much on one brain level. For example, when we act mainly from the first brain, we react from instinct alone with no thought given to the consequences. When this happens, we do not consider how someone else may feel, and our actions may get us into trouble. At other times, we may act primarily from the second brain. In this case, unmanaged emotions can play too strong a role in our decisions and behavior. We can keep worrying about something that is not really worth it or get angry over a situation when we do not have all the facts. For example, rumor has it that your boyfriend said something about your best friend that was not true. If you'd bother to ask what he really said, you might find out that it wasn't what he said at all. Sometimes, we get mad first and ask questions later.

If the second and third brains are not working together well, we may not even know what we are feeling, yet the feelings can drive our actions and affect our thoughts and decisions. For instance, with your third brain, you know you need to work on your science report, but you choose to watch TV instead. During the show, you can't quite relax and enjoy yourself. You're anxious about the report, though you may not admit it. An important aspect of growing into adulthood is getting the second and third brains to work together harmoniously. The second brain involves acting on our impulses and emotions, sometimes without much awareness of how our feelings are affecting us. The third brain allows us to gain more power to control our impulses and emotions. We see more clearly what is meaningful to us in life and make our choices based on these values. As we've already said, the third brain provides foresight that allows us to see ahead, so we are able to consider the consequences of our decisions before acting. However, when we are operating mostly from the third brain, we can get trapped in "looping thoughts" that lead to excessive worry and anxiety.

Emotions and Human Behavior

Inbar and Avramova (2013) observe that "morality pervades human society. Some of the earliest preserved writings of Greek philosophers are on the quintessentially moral topic of justice. Our oldest and most cherished texts, religious and otherwise, concern themselves largely with moral questions—what to do or avoid doing; what distinguishes the righteous from the wicked." Lerner, Li, Valdesolo & Kassam (2014) present a number of scientific inquiries regarding how emotions influence human behavior.

Integral Emotions

We start with emotions arising from the judgment or choice at hand (i.e., integral emotion), a type of emotion that strongly and routinely shapes decision-making (Damasio 1994, Greene & Haidt 2002). For example, a person who feels anxious about the potential outcome of a risky choice may choose a safer option rather than a potentially more lucrative option. A person who feels grateful for a school they attended may decide to donate a large sum to that school even though it limits personal spending. Such effects of integral emotions operate at conscious and non-conscious levels.

Integral emotion as a beneficial guide

Although a negative view of emotion's role in reason has dominated much of Western thought (Keltner & Lerner 2010), a few philosophers pioneered the idea that integral emotion could be a beneficial guide. David Hume (1738/1978, p.415), for example, argued that the dominant predisposition toward viewing emotion as secondary to reason is entirely backward: "Reason is, and ought only to be, the slave of the passions, and can never pretend to any other office than to serve and obey them." Following this view, anger, for example, provides the motivation to respond to injustice (Solomon 1993), and anticipation of regret provides a reason to avoid excessive risk-taking (Loomes & Sugden 1982).

Compelling scientific evidence for this view comes from emotionally impaired patients who have sustained injuries to the ventromedial prefrontal cortex (vmPFC), a key area of the brain for integrating emotion and cognition. Studies find that such neurological impairments reduce both patients' ability to feel the emotion and the optimality of their decisions in ways that cannot be explained by simple cognitive changes (Bechara et al. 1999, Damasio 1994). Participants with vmPFC injuries repeatedly select a riskier financial option over a safer one, even to the point of bankruptcy—despite their cognitive understanding of the sub-optimality of their choices. Physiological measures of galvanic skin response suggest that this behavior is due to these participants not experiencing the emotional signals — "somatic markers" — that lead normal decision-makers to have a reasonable fear of high risks.

Integral emotion as bias
Despite arising from the judgment or decision at hand, integral emotions can also degrade decision making. For example, one may feel afraid to fly and decide to drive instead, even though base rates for death by driving are much higher than base rates for death by flying the equivalent mileage (Gigerenzer 2004). Integral emotions can be remarkably influential even in the presence of cognitive information that would suggest alternative courses of action (for review, see Loewenstein 1996). Once integral emotions attach themselves to decision targets, they become difficult to detach (Rozin et al. 1986). Prior reviews have described myriad ways in which integral emotional inputs to decision-making, especially perceptually vivid ones, can override otherwise rational courses of action (Loewenstein et al. 2001).

Incidental Emotions' Influence on Decision-Making

Researchers have found that incidental emotions pervasively carry over from one situation to the next, affecting decisions that should, from a normative perspective, be unrelated to that emotion (for selective reviews, Han et al. 2007, Keltner & Lerner 2010, Lerner& Keltner 2000, Lerner & Tiedens 2006, Loewenstein & Lerner 2003, Pham 2007, Vohs et al. 2007, Yates 2007), a process called the carryover of incidental emotion (Bodenhausen 1993, Loewenstein & Lerner 2003). For example, incidental anger triggered in one situation automatically elicits a motive to blame individuals in other situations even though the targets of such anger have nothing to do with the source of the anger (Quigley & Tedeschi 1996). Moreover, the carryover of incidental emotions typically occurs without awareness.

Incidental emotion as Psychological bias models have begun to elucidate the mechanisms through which the carryover effect occurs as well as the moderators that amplify or attenuate the effect. Early studies of carryover either implicitly or explicitly took a valence-based approach, dividing emotions into positive and negative categories, and posting that emotions of the same valence would have similar effects: people in good moods would make optimistic judgments, and people in bad moods would make pessimistic judgments (for reviews, see Han et al. 2007, Keltner & Lerner 2010, Loewenstein & Lerner 2003).

Using a valence-grounded approach, Johnson and Tversky (1983) conducted the first empirical demonstration of incidental affect's influence upon risk perception. Participants read newspaper stories designed to induce positive or negative affect and then estimated fatality frequencies for various potential causes of death (e.g., heart disease). Compared to participants who read positive stories, participants who read negative stories offered pessimistic estimates of fatalities. Surprisingly, the influence of mood on judgment did not depend on the similarity between the content of stories and the content of subsequent judgments. Rather, the mood itself generally affected all judgments.

Research in economics has recently begun to study incidental emotion carryover at the macro level. For example, based on the assumption that people are happier on sunny days, economists found a positive correlation between the amount of sunshine on a given day and stock market performance across 26 countries (Hirshleifer & Shumway 2003, Kamstra et al. 2003). In contrast, stock market returns declined when a country's soccer team was eliminated from the World Cup (Edmans et al. 2007). These studies make a promising connection between micro-level and macro-level phenomena that should increase in precision as promising new methods emerge for measuring public mood and emotion (e.g. Bollen et al. 2011), as well as individual subjective experiences across time and situations (Barrett & Barrett 2001, Stayman & Aaker 1993), within psychology.

Moderating factors

The field is just starting to identify moderating factors for the carryover of incidental emotion. One promising line of work is Forgas's (1995) Affect Infusion Model, which elaborates on the circumstances under which affect—integral and/or incidental—influences social judgment. The model predicts that the degree of affect infusion into judgments varies along a processing continuum, such that effect is most likely to influence the judgment in complex and unanticipated situations. Another promising line is the emerging hypothesis by Yip and Côté (2013), which predicts that individuals with high emotional intelligence can correctly identify which events caused their emotions and, therefore, can screen out the potential impact of incidental emotion. In one study, individuals high in emotion-understanding ability showed less impact of incidental anxiety on risk estimates when informed about the incidental source of their anxiety. Although solid evidence supports both of these emerging approaches to mapping moderators, the field needs much more attention to moderators in order to understand how emotion and decision-making processes occur in the varied private and public settings in which decisions are made.

Beyond Valence: Specific Emotions Influence Decision Making

The earliest literature on emotion and judgment and decision-making implicitly or explicitly took a valence-based approach, but such models cannot account for all influences of affect upon judgment and choice. Though parsimonious, valence models sacrifice specificity by overlooking evidence that emotions of the same valence differ in essential ways. For example, the emotions of the same valence, such as anger and sadness, are associated with different antecedent appraisals (Smith & Ellsworth 1985); depths of processing (Bodenhausen et al. 1994b); brain hemispheric activation (Harmon-Jones & Sigelman 2001); facial expressions (Ekman 2007); autonomic responses (Levenson et al. 1990); and central nervous system activity (Phelps et al. in press). At least as far back as 1998, an Annual Review of Psychology on JDM noted the insufficiency of valence and arousal in predicting JDM outcomes: "Even a two-dimensional model seems inadequate for describing emotional experiences. Anger, sadness, and disgust are all forms of negative affect, and arousal does not capture all of the differences among them... A more detailed approach is required to understand the relationships between emotions and decisions (Mellers et al. 1998, p.454)."

In an effort to increase the predictive power and precision of JDM models of emotion, Lerner and Keltner (2000, 2001) proposed examining multi-dimensional discrete emotions with the Appraisal-Tendency Framework (ATF). The ATF systematically links the appraisal processes associated with specific emotions to different judgment and choice outcomes. The general approach predicts that emotions of the same valence (such as fear and anger) can exert distinct influences on choices and judgments, while emotions of the opposite valence (such as anger and happiness) can exert similar influences.

The ATF rests on three broad assumptions: (a) that a discrete set of cognitive dimensions differentiates emotional experience (e.g., Ellsworth & Smith 1988, Lazarus 1991, Ortony et al. 1988, Scherer 1999, Smith & Ellsworth 1985); (b) that emotions serve a coordination role, automatically triggering a set of concomitant responses (physiology, behavior, experience, and communication) that enable the individual to quickly deal with problems or opportunities (e.g., Frijda 1988, Levenson 1994, Oatley & Jenkins 1992); and (c) that emotions have motivational properties that depend on both an emotion's intensity and its qualitative character, that is, specific emotions carry specific "action tendencies" (e.g., Frijda 1986), or implicit goals that signal the most adaptive response. In this view, emotions save cognitive processing by triggering time-tested, responses to universal experiences (such as loss, injustice, and threat) (Levenson 1994, Tooby & Cosmides 1990). For example, anger triggers aggression, and fear triggers flight. Lazarus (1991) has argued that each emotion is associated with a "core-relational," or appraisal theme—the central relational harm or benefit that underlies each specific emotion. The ATF points to a clear empirical strategy: Research should compare emotions that are highly differentiated in their appraisal themes on judgments and choices that relate to that appraisal theme (Lerner & Keltner 2000). Han and colleagues (2007) refer to this strategy as the "matching principle," which we discuss further in the next section. By illuminating the cognitive and motivational processes associated with different emotions, the model provides a flexible yet specific framework for developing a host of testable hypotheses concerning effect and JDM. The appraisal-tendency hypothesis states that appraisal tendencies are goal-directed processes through which emotions exert effects upon judgments and decisions until the emotion-eliciting problem is resolved (Lerner & Keltner 2000, Lerner & Keltner 2001). The ATF predicts that an emotion, once activated, can trigger a cognitive predisposition to assess future events in line with the central appraisal dimensions that triggered the emotion (for example, see Table 1).

Such appraisals become an implicit perceptual lens for interpreting subsequent situations. Just as emotions include action tendencies that predispose individuals to act in specific ways to meet environmental problems and opportunities (e.g. Frijda 1986), the ATF posits that emotions predispose individuals to appraise the environment in specific ways toward similar functional ends. An early study consistent with the ATF examined the effects of anger and sadness upon causal attributions (Keltner et al. 1993). Although both anger and sadness have a negative valence, appraisals of individual control characterize anger, whereas appraisals of situational control characterize sadness. The authors predicted that these differences would drive attributions of responsibility for subsequent events. Consistent with this hypothesis, incidental anger increased attributions of individual responsibility for life outcomes, whereas incidental sadness increased the tendency to perceive fate or situational circumstances as responsible for life outcomes.

In an explicit test of the ATF, Lerner and Keltner (2000) compared risk perceptions of fearful and angry people. Consistent with the ATF, dispositional fearful people made pessimistic judgments of future events, whereas dispositional angry people were optimistic. Subsequent experimental studies induced participants to feel incidental anger or fear and found identical results (Lerner & Keltner 2001). Importantly, participants' appraisals of certainty and control mediated the causal effects of fear and anger on optimism. Findings consistent with the ATF in many other contexts have further supported this approach (for discussion, see Bagneux et al. 2012, Cavanaugh et al. 2007, Han et al. 2007, Horberg et al. 2011, Lerner & Tiedens 2006, Yates 2007). For example, one study challenged a valence-based tendency for people in positive moods to make positive judgments and vice versa for negative moods, finding differential effects of sadness and anger on judgments of likelihood, despite both emotions having a negative valence (DeSteno et al. 2000). DeSteno and colleagues have also shown several ways in which positive emotions predict behavior beyond the contributions of valence (Bartlett & DeSteno 2006, Williams & DeSteno 2008). For example, several studies show that specific positive emotions, such as gratitude and pride, have unique effects on helping behavior and task perseverance. Others have delineated the unique profiles of various positive states in accordance with differences in their appraisal themes (Campos & Keltner in press, Valdesolo & Graham 2014).

Emotions Shape Decisions via the Content of Thought

Given that discrete emotions are grounded in cognitive appraisals (for review, see Keltner & Lerner 2010), the ATF helps identify the effects of specific emotions on judgment and choice, breaking down emotions into cognitive dimensions that can be mapped onto the content of thought JDM processes. A number of these appraisal dimensions involve themes that have been central to JDM research: the perceived likelihood of various events, economic valuation, and assignment of responsibility and causality. Consider two illustrations of how emotions shape the content of thought via appraisal tendencies, drawn from Lerner and Keltner (2000). The ATF predicts that dimensions on which emotion scores particularly low or high are likely to activate an appraisal tendency that influences JDM, even for incidental emotions. Anger scores high on the dimensions of certainty, control, and others' responsibility, and low on pleasantness. These characteristics suggest that angry people will view negative events as predictably caused by and under the control of other individuals.

In contrast, fear involves low certainty and a low sense of control, which are likely to produce a perception of negative events as unpredictable and situationally determined. These differences in appraisal tendencies are particularly relevant to risk perception, with fearful people tending to see greater risk and angry people tending to see less risk. As described above, correlation and experimental work supports this idea (Lerner & Keltner 2000, Lerner & Keltner 2001). A match between the appraisal themes of a specific emotion and the particular domain of a judgment or decision predict the likelihood that a given emotion will influence a given judgment or decision.

Differences in appraisal dimensions of pride and surprise, meanwhile, suggest different effects on attributions of responsibility. Specifically, pride scores lower than surprise on the dimension of others' responsibility, whereas surprise scores low on certainty. These differences suggest that pride will produce an appraisal tendency to attribute favorable events to one's own efforts, whereas surprise will produce an appraisal tendency to see favorable events as unpredictable and outside one's own control. These differences are likely to be relevant to judgments of attribution, with pride increasing perceptions of one's own responsibility for positive events and surprise increasing perceptions of others' responsibility for positive events, even when the judgment is unrelated to the source of the pride or surprise.

An experiment conducted in the wake of the 9/11 terrorist attacks tested whether these patterns would scale up to the population level. A nationally representative sample of U.S. citizens read either a real news story (on the threat of anthrax) selected to elicit fear or a real news story (on celebrations of the attacks by some people in Arab countries) selected to elicit anger, and then were asked a series of questions about perceived risks and policy preferences (Lerner et al. 2003). Participants induced with fear perceived greater risk in the world, whereas those induced with anger perceived lower risk, both for events related and unrelated to terrorism. Participants in the anger condition also supported harsher policies against suspected terrorists than did participants in the fear condition.

Emotions Shape the Depth of Thought

In addition to the content of thought, emotions also influence the depth of information processing related to decision making. As with other emotion research, early studies focused on the effects of positive and negative moods (Schwarz 1990, Schwarz & Bless 1991). If emotions serve an adaptive role by signaling when a situation demands additional attention, they hypothesized, then negative mood should signal threat and thus increase vigilant systematic processing, and positive mood should signal a safe environment and lead to more heuristic processing. Indeed, numerous studies have shown that people in positive or negative affective states were respectively more or less influenced by heuristic cues, such as the expertise, attractiveness, or likeability of the source, and the length rather than the quality of the message while also relying more on stereotypes (Bless et al. 1996, Bodenhausen et al. 1994a). Note that systematic processing is not necessarily more desirable than automatic processing. Studies have shown that increased systematic processing from negative affect can aggravate anchoring effects due to an increased focus on the anchor (Bodenhausen et al. 2000). Similarly, negative affect reduces the accuracy of thin-sliced judgments of teacher effectiveness except when participants were under cognitive load, suggesting that the accuracy decrease for sad participants was caused by more deliberative processing (Ambady & Gray 2002).

Finally, dysphoric people show excessive rumination (Lyubomirsky & Nolen-Hoeksema 1995). Although this research shows clear influences of effect on processing depth, it has typically operationalized positive affect as happiness and negative affect as sadness. In one exception, Bodenhausen and colleagues (1994b) compared the effects of sadness and anger, both negatively balanced emotions. Relative to neutral or sad participants, angry participants showed a greater reliance on stereotypic judgments and heuristic cues, inconsistent with valence-based explanations but consistent with the affect-as-information view that anger carries positive information about one's own position (Clore et al. 2001).

Tiedens and Linton (2001) suggested an alternative explanation for the difference between happiness and sadness in depth of processing: happiness involves appraisals of high certainty and sadness of low certainty. A series of four studies showed that high-certainty emotions (e.g., happiness, anger, disgust) increased heuristic processing by increasing reliance on the sourcing expertise of a persuasive message as opposed to its content, increasing usage of stereotypes, and decreasing attention to argument quality. Further, manipulating certainty appraisals independently from emotion showed that certainty plays a causal role in determining whether people engage in heuristic or systematic processing.

Since Lerner and Tiedens (2006) introduced emotion effects on depth of thought into the ATF framework, studies have shown emotion influences on the depth of processing across numerous domains. For example, Small and Lerner (2008) found that, relative to neutral-state participants, angry participants allocated less to welfare recipients, and sad participants allocated more. This effect was eliminated under cognitive load, suggesting that allocations were predicted by differences in depth of processing between sad and angry participants.

Emotions Shape Decisions via Goal Activation
It has been argued that emotions serve an adaptive coordination role, triggering a set of responses (physiology, behavior, experience, and communication) that enable individuals to deal quickly with encountered problems or opportunities (for review, see Keltner et al. 2014). For example, in their investigation of action tendencies, Frijda and colleagues (1989) found that anger was associated with the desire to change the situation and "move against" another person or obstacle by fighting, harming, or conquering it. As one would expect, readiness to fight manifests not only experientially but also physiologically. For example, anger is associated with neural activation characteristics of approach motivation (Harmon-Jones & Sigelman 2001) and sometimes with changes in peripheral physiology that might prepare one to fight, such as increased blood flow to the hands (Ekman & Davidson 1994). Emotion-specific action tendencies map onto appraisal themes. For example, given that anxiety is characterized by the appraisal theme of facing uncertain

25

existential threats (Lazarus 1991), it accompanies the action tendency to reduce uncertainty (Raghunathan & Pham 1999). Sadness, by contrast, is characterized by the appraisal theme of experiencing an irrevocable loss (Lazarus 1991) and thus accompanies the action tendency to change one's circumstances, perhaps by seeking rewards (Lerner et al. 2004). Consistent with this logic, a set of studies contrasted the effects of incidental anxiety and sadness on hypothetical gambling and job-selection decisions and found that sadness increased tendencies to favor high-risk, high-reward options, whereas anxiety increased tendencies to favor low-risk, low-reward options (Raghunathan & Pham 1999).

Lerner and colleagues (2004) followed a similar logic in a series of studies that tested the effects of incidental sadness and disgust on the endowment effect (Kahneman et al. 1991), whereby sellers value goods more than buyers do because sellers see the sale as a loss of ownership. The authors hypothesized that disgust, which revolves around the appraisal theme of being too close to a potentially contaminating object (Lazarus 1991), would evoke an implicit goal to expel current objects and avoid taking in anything new (Rozin et al. 2008). Consistent with this hypothesis, experimentally-induced incidental disgust reduced selling prices among participants who owned the experimental object (an "expel" goal) and reduced buying prices among participants who did not (an "avoid taking anything in" goal). For sadness, associated with the appraisal themes of loss and misfortune, both selling old goods and buying new goods present opportunities to change one's circumstances. Consistent with predictions, sadness reduced selling prices but increased buying prices. In sum, incidental disgust eliminated the endowment effect, whereas incidental sadness reversed it.

Han and colleagues (2012) further tested the effects of disgust on implicit goals in the context of the status-quo bias, a preference for keeping a current option over switching to another option (Samuelson & Zeckhauser 1988), and ruled out more general valence- or arousal-based disgust effects. A valence-based account would predict that any negative emotion should devalue all choice options, preserving status-quo bias (Forgas 2003). An arousal-based account would predict disgust to exacerbate status-quo bias by amplifying the dominant response option (Foster et al. 1998). In contrast, an implicit goals-based account would predict disgust to trigger a goal of expelling the current option. Data support this last interpretation. Given the choice between keeping one generic box of unspecified office supplies (the status quo) or switching to another generic box of similar but unspecified office supplies, disgust-state participants were significantly more likely than neutral-state participants to switch. As is commonly the case with effects of incidental emotion, the effects of disgust on choices eluded participants' awareness. Lerner and colleagues (2013) tested whether the effect of sadness on implicit goals would increase impatience in financial decisions, creating a myopic focus on obtaining money immediately instead of obtaining it later, even if immediate rewards were much smaller than later awards. As predicted, relative to median neutral-state participants, median sad-state participants across studies accepted 13% to 34% less money immediately to avoid waiting three months for payment. Again, valence-based accounts cannot explain this effect: disgusted participants were just as patient as neutral participants. The view that discrete emotions trigger discrete implicit goals is consistent with the "Feeling is for doing" model (Zeelenberg et al. 2008), a theoretical framework asserting that the behaviors define the adaptive function of emotion that specific states motivate. According to Zeelenberg and colleagues, these motivational orientations derive from the experiential qualities of such emotions, as opposed to, for example, the appraisal tendencies giving rise to their experience. Thus, the behavioral effects depend only on the perceived relevance of an emotion to a current goal, regardless of whether the emotion is integral or incidental to the decision at hand. Given that the ATF does not distinguish informational versus experiential pathways, an important agenda for future work is to develop more granular evidence of the mechanisms through which emotions activate implicit goals in judgment and choice. At present, the models appear to make similar predictions.

Emotions Influence Interpersonal Decision Making

Emotions are inherently social (for review, see Keltner & Lerner 2010), and a full explanation of their adaptive utility requires an understanding of their reciprocal influence on interaction partners. As an example of how complex such influences can be, people derive happiness merely from opportunities to help and give to others with no expectation of concrete gains (Dunn et al. 2008). Indeed, prosociality is sometimes used instrumentally to manage one's mood, relieving sadness or distress (Schaller & Cialdini 1988).

Emotions help optimally navigate social decisions. Scholars have conceptualized emotions as communication systems that help people navigate and coordinate social interactions by providing information about others' motives and dispositions, ultimately allowing for creating and maintaining healthy and productive social relationships (Keltner et al. 2014, Morris & Keltner 2000). In the case of psychopathology (e.g., narcissism), emotions impede healthy and productive social relationships (Kring 2008). Frank (1988) argues that the communicative function of emotions has played a crucial role in helping people solve important commitment problems raised by mixed motives. That is, whether we decide to pursue cooperative or competitive strategies with others depends on our beliefs about their intentions (c.f. Singer & Fehr 2005), information that is often inferred from their emotions (Fessler 2007). This approach has been particularly evident in the study of mixed-motive situations (e.g., negotiation and bargaining; c.f. Van Kleef et al. 2010). For example, communicating gratitude triggers others' generosity (Rind & Bordia 1995) and ultimately helps an individual build social and economic capital (DeSteno 2009). Latest research leads to the conclusion that emotion may serve at least three functions in interpersonal decision making: (a) helping individuals understand one another's emotions, beliefs, and intentions; (b) incentivizing or imposing a cost on others' behavior; and (c) evoking complementary, reciprocal, or shared emotions in others (Keltner & Haidt 1999). For example, expressions of anger prompt concessions from negotiation partners (Van Kleef et al. 2004a) and more cooperative strategies in bargaining games (Van Dijk et al. 2008) because anger signals a desire for behavioral adjustment (Fischer& Roseman 2007). This effect is qualified by contextual variables, such as the motivation and ability of interaction partners to process emotional information (Van Kleef et al. 2004b) as well as the morally charged nature of a negotiation (Dehghani et al. in press). Multi-party negotiations show different effects; for example, communicated anger can lead to exclusion in these contexts (Van Beest et al. 2008).

One study investigating this mechanism found that people seem to use others' emotional displays to make inferences about their appraisals and, subsequently, their mental states (de Melo et al. 2014). Discrete supplication emotions (disappointment or worry) evoke higher concessions from negotiators as compared to similarly-valenced appeasement emotions (guilt or regret; Van Kleef et al. 2006). As compared to anger, disappointment also engenders more cooperation. For instance, in the "give-some game" (Wubben et al. 2009), two participants simultaneously decide how much money to give to the other participant or keep for themselves. Any money given is doubled, and this procedure is repeated over 14 trials. After perceived failures of reciprocity, expressing disappointment communicates a forgiving nature and motivates greater cooperation, whereas expressing anger communicates a retaliatory nature and promotes an escalation of defection. Though interpersonal emotions can influence others' behavior by communicating information about an emoter's intentions, they can also change decisions and behavior as a function of the corresponding or complementary emotional states they evoke in others. Anger can elicit fear when communicated by those high in power or corresponding anger when communicated by those low in power (Lelieveld et al. 2012) and also a desire for retaliation (Wang et al. 2012). Communicating disappointment with a proposal can evoke guilt in a bargaining partner and motivate reparative action (Lelieveld et al. 2013). Decision-makers try to use the emotional communications of bargaining partners as sources of strategic information (Andrade & Ho 2007). Increasing knowledge of how emotion communication influences others' decisions also raises the possibility of the strategic display of emotional expression.

The few studies investigating this possibility have produced mixed results: Though such strategies can prompt greater concessions (Kopelman et al. 2006), inauthentic displays that are detected are met with increased demands and reduced trust (Côté et al. 2013). The costs and benefits of intentionally deploying emotional expressions in such contexts will be an interesting area for future research. For example, initial work (Elfenbein et al. 2007, Mueller & Curhan 2006) suggests that emotionally intelligent individuals, for example, should be better able to elicit desired emotions from counterparts and, therefore, might use such skills to achieve desired outcomes. Emotion influences group processes and perceptions of groups. Research on group-level emotional processes is surprisingly scant, given that so many high-stakes decisions are made in groups and that the existing research reveals important effects. For example, research has found that, although team members tend to feel happy and to enjoy groups that have a shared sense of reality, such feelings are associated with groupthink—the destructive tendency to minimize conflict and maximize harmony and conformity (Janis 1972). Given that general positivity or negativity can spread through groups and influence performance outcomes (e.g., Barsade 2002, Hatfield et al. 1993, Totterdell 2000), more research in this area is considerably needed, especially at the level of specific emotions.

Unwanted Effects of Emotion on Decision Making can Sometimes Be Reduced

Although emotion's influences on JDM are not always harmful and are sometimes even helpful, a number of strategies have examined ways to minimize the deleterious effects of emotions on decision making. These strategies broadly take one of two forms: (a) minimizing the magnitude of the emotional response (e.g., through time delay, reappraisal, or inducing a counteracting emotional state), or (b) insulating the judgment or decision process from the emotion (e.g., by crowding out emotion, increasing awareness of misattribution, or modifying the choice architecture).

Solutions that seek to minimize the emotional response
Time Delay

Time delay, in theory, being the simplest strategy for minimizing emotional magnitude is to let time pass before making a decision. Emotions are short-lived (Levenson 1994). Facial expressions are fleeting (Keltner et al. 2003), and physiological responses quickly fade (e.g., Mauss et al. 2005). The extensive literature on affective forecasting has documented the surprising power of adaptation and rationalization to bring our emotional states back toward baseline even after traumatic events (c.f. Wilson & Gilbert 2005). In certain instances, perhaps rare ones, induced anger may cause immediate changes in participants' decisions but show no such effects when the induction and decision are separated by a 10-minute delay (Gneezy & Imas 2014). Anyone who has ever observed a family member nursing a grudge for years may question the boundary conditions of time delay. In short, although it cannot be said that time heals all wounds, research in psychology has revealed that humans revert back to baseline states over time, an effect we typically underestimate (Gilbert 2006, Loewenstein 2000).

That said, there is a reason why a strategy as simple as waiting is so rarely used. The reason: delay is fundamentally antithetical to the function of many emotional states, which motivate behavioral responses to immediate adaptive concerns. Few would disagree that taking a moment to decide how to react after discovering a spouse in the arms of another would be prudent. Fewer still would actually be capable of doing so. The immediate effects of emotional states can render us "out of control" and incapable of waiting for a neutral state to return (Loewenstein 1996).

Suppression

Although suppression is often touted in the popular literature (e.g., "control your anger"), research indicates that it is often counterproductive, intensifying the very emotional state one had hoped to regulate (Wenzlaff & Wegner 2000). Attempting to avoid feeling an emotion will typically reduce one's expressive behavior but have little or no impact on one's subjective experience of the emotion (Gross & Levenson 1993). Indeed, physiological reactions to suppression are often mixed and frequently deleterious (Gross 2002, Gross & Levenson 1993). Specifically, attempts at suppression are cognitively costly, impairing memory for details of what triggered the emotion (Richards & Gross 1999). This effect has important practical implications for how individuals might best respond to unexpected accidents that trigger intense emotion.

Reappraisal

Reframing the meaning of stimuli that led to an emotional response, i.e., reappraisal, has consistently emerged as a superior strategy for dissipating the emotional response (Gross 2002). Reappraisal includes such behaviors as reminding oneself "it's just a test" after receiving a poor exam grade, adopting the mindset of a nurse or medical professional to minimize the emotional impact of viewing someone's injury, or viewing a job layoff as an opportunity to pursue long-forgotten dreams (Gross 1998, Gross 2002). In contrast to suppression, reappraisal not only reduces self-reported negative feelings in response to negative events but also mitigates physiological and neural responses to those events (Jamieson et al. 2012, Ochsner et al. 2002). Those who employ strategic reappraisal typically have more positive emotional experiences (Gross & John 2003) and show fewer incidences of psychopathology (Aldao et al. 2010).

As yet, we find few studies applying reappraisal techniques to emotion effects on JDM, but one path-breaking paper suggests that this area holds promise. Halperin and colleagues (2012) examined the responses of Israelis to the recent Palestinian bid for United Nations recognition. Participants who were randomly assigned to a reappraisal training condition (compared to a control condition) showed greater support for conciliatory policies and less support for aggressive policies toward Palestinians at planned assessments both one week and five months later.

The relative efficacy of suppression and reappraisal techniques derives from the content of thoughts about emotions, i.e., "don't think about this", or "think about this differently". A separate literature on mood repair suggests the possibility of another route to regulation: triggering other target emotional states that "cancel out" the original state.

The "two-state solution" (inducing a counteracting emotional state)

Theoretically, one could counteract an unwanted decision effect by inducing another emotion—one that triggers opposing tendencies in JDM. Thus, the decision process would still involve bias, but the decision outcome would not. A provocative example of this approach examined the well-known phenomenon of excessively high financial discount rates, as described in the JDM primer. Whereas sadness is known to increase excessive discount rates (Lerner et al. 2013), gratitude has now been shown to reduce such rates, even below levels one would experience in a neutral state (DeSteno et al. 2014). These results suggest the unusual possibility that inducing an incidental emotion (in this case, gratitude) may reduce an existing bias. Akin to (Loewenstein et al. 2012), one might use one bias to counteract another.

Approaches that Seek to Insulate the Decision Process from the Emotion—Increasing cognitive effort through financial incentives

Few studies have systematically tested ways to reduce the carryover of incidental emotion; results to date suggest that such reduction will be difficult.Increasing a decision maker's attention to the decision task by having real financial outcomes is often considered a good way to reduce bias, but this intuition does not seem to be effective. Incidental emotions routinely serve as perceptual lenses even when real financial rewards are at stake (e.g., DeSteno et al. 2014, Lerner et al. 2013, Lerner et al. 2004, Loewenstein et al. 2001).

Crowding out emotion

Saturating the decision-maker with cognitive facts about a particular decision domain and making the domain-relevant might also seem like useful ways to diminish the carryover effect. Unfortunately, neither strategy appears promising. For example, although U.S. citizens paid close attention to risk and safety matters in the wake of 9/11, incidental emotions induced shortly after the attacks shaped citizens' global perceptions of risk and their preferences for risky courses of action (Lerner et al. 2003).

Increasing awareness of misattribution

Based on the idea that emotion-related appraisals are automatic (Ekman 1992, Lazarus 1991, LeDoux 1996), the "cognitive-awareness hypothesis" (Han et al. 2007) posits that appraisal tendencies will be deactivated when decision-makers become more cognitively aware of their decision-making process. Schwarz and Clore (1983) pioneered this approach, discovering in a seminal study that ambient weather effects on judgments of subjective well-being disappeared when people were reminded of the weather. In a similar vein, Lerner and colleagues (1998) showed that inducing decision-makers to monitor their judgment processes in a preemptively self-critical way, via the expectation that they would need to justify their decisions to an expert audience, i.e., accountability, reduced the impact of incidental anger on punishment decisions by leading people to focus on judgment-relevant information and dismiss incidental affect as irrelevant to the judgment. Notably, the accountable decision-makers did not feel any less anger than the non-accountable decision-makers; they simply used better judgment cues. It should be noted that these examples of deactivation of emotional carryover may be more the exception than the rule, as numerous factors can thwart cognitive awareness. First, people often lack the motivation to monitor their decision-making process. Moreover, even when people are motivated, attaining accurate awareness of their decision processes is a difficult task (for review, see Wilson & Brekke 1994). For example, incidental disgust led participants to get rid of their possessions even when they were directly warned to avoid this carryover effect of disgust (Han et al. 2012).

Stepping back to consider broader frameworks for organizing and understanding bias in JDM, the type of incidental emotion carryover observed appears most consistent with what Wilson and Brekke (1994) refer to as "mental contamination" and Arkes (1991) calls "association-based errors"—processes wherein bias (e.g., incidental emotion carryover) arises because of mental processing that is unconscious or uncontrollable. These models suggest that the best strategy for reducing such biases would be to control one's exposure to biased information in the first place. This is a difficult task for the decision-maker. Thus, debiasing may be more effectively accomplished by altering the structure of the choice context. In this chapter, we have extensively examined the subject matter of emotions and how they influence human behavior. We have also seen several proposed theories of how to control the impact of emotions on decision making. Although emotions may arise from our internal environment, they often also arise from our external environment – the things we see, hear and read. If this is so, how can we minimize the impact of negative input from the environment on the state of our hearts?

CHAPTER THREE

HEART AND MIND CONNECTION

*A*ll human body parts are crucial for our survival, but if we rank each organ's importance in our body, then the brain and the heart may likely be at the top. Also, whenever we talk about our spiritual makeup, the heart as well as the mind seemed to top the list too. But is there any difference between the two? What is the relationship between the heart and the mind? We can look into the Bible to address these questions.

The Difference Between the Heart and Mind
When you take a look at the Bible, you will discover that the heart and mind were mentioned thousands of times. When we go through various Bible passages that talk about the heart and mind, we will encounter many different definitions for the heart and the mind depending on the way each of the words were used in various contexts.

Generally, as discussed above, the heart has to do with the part of humans that controls the emotions, dreams, desires, hopes, and other intangible aspects of our being. On the other hand, the mind typically has to do with the part of humans that controls reason, intellect, and thoughts.

The Importance of the Heart and Mind for Biblical Faith
According to Ephesians 2:8; (JKV) "For it is by grace you have been saved, through faith—and this is not from yourselves, it is the gift of God." The Bible makes it clear that we are saved through faith. So, our mind and heart need to be engaged in this process because to have faith in God means to believe and trust God.

Believing requires the mind, and in order to trust someone, we need the heart. We are saved when we believe certain facts about God. He sent his son Jesus Christ into this world, and his son died on the cross for our sins. Jesus Christ was raised from the dead on the third day, and He ascended into heaven. God sent the Holy Spirit to dwell in anyone who believes in Jesus Christ. These are some of the essential facts that every Christian must believe.

However, if our faith ends with the mind's beliefs, then it is not the saving faith. James 2:19; "You believe that there is one God. Good! Even the demons believe that—and shudder." This implies that even Satan believes the truth about God in his mind, but Satan does not live for God and does not trust God. James further explained that faith without works is dead, which means that if we simply believe certain parts, it does not make our faith genuine because genuine faith affects how we live our lives. If truly we trust God, then our life will only be lived for him.

There is a need to believe and trust in order to have saving faith, and this requires the "mind and the heart." Therefore, the heart and mind need to be transformed by the power of the Holy Spirit as is written in I Corinthians 2:6-16, "We do, however, speak a message of wisdom among the mature, but not the wisdom of this age or of the rulers of this age, who are coming to nothing. No, we declare God's wisdom, a mystery that has been hidden and that God destined for our glory before time began. None of the rulers of this age understood it, for if they had, they would not have crucified the Lord of glory. However, as it is written: "What no eye has seen, what no ear has heard, and what no human mind has conceived" [a]—the things God has prepared for those who love him — these are the things God has revealed to us by his Spirit. The Spirit searches all things, even the deep things of God... Who has known the mind of the Lord so as to instruct him?" But we have the mind of Christ.

Also, Ezekiel 36:26-27; "I will give you a new heart and put a new spirit in you; I will remove from you your heart of stone and give you a heart of flesh. 27 And I will put my Spirit in you and move you to follow my decrees and be careful to keep my laws." All those that genuinely know God will undoubtedly love God with all their heart and mind.

The Heart and Mind and our Relationship with God

If you must have an intimate relationship with God, then you will need to engage your heart. Also, if you must have a true relationship with God, then you must engage your mind. It is possible for you to passionately worship your version of God and even lifelessly believe in a doctrinally accurate picture of God. But what God desires from us is to love him truly and passionately.

You must understand that the more passionately we love God as a person, the more we will learn to know the truth about him. The more truth we learn about God while studying the Bible, the more we will passionately love him. Remember, as humans, the way we feel actually affects the way we think and the way we think has a great influence on the way we feel.

In Philippians 4:4-7; "Rejoice in the Lord always. I will say it again: Rejoice! Let your gentleness be evident to all. The Lord is near. Do not be anxious about anything, but in every situation, by prayer and petition, with thanksgiving, present your requests to God. And the peace of God, which transcends all understanding, will guard your hearts and your minds in Christ Jesus." [Highlighted by me] This Bible passage clearly illustrates our relationship with God. It explains that we must rejoice (this is an emotion of the heart) because God is near (this is an intellectual fact). It explains that we must be reasonable (the mind), we shouldn't be anxious (the heart); we need to pray concerning specific things in specific ways (this will require our mind). So, when we are able to do this, then a peace that surpasses understanding will rest upon us (this is what we will feel in our hearts).

Generally, when we are in a relationship with God, the Bible makes it clear that Jesus Christ will affect our heart and mind; Psalm 119:169-176 (ESV). These Bible verses clearly talk about engaging our heart and mind; we must "cry," "understand," "pour forth praise," etc. All the phrases swing between passion and intellect, rules and help, understanding and desire. The passion of the psalmist (in the heart) is rooted in Biblical knowledge (the mind). His statement: "My lips will pour forth praise" (from the heart), for you teach me your statutes (the mind)." So, it is clear that the heart and mind control various aspects of our existence. However, they are connected. The two are required in advancing the relationship we have with God as well as our love for Him.

Christian faith requires knowledge and trust, and there is no way we can trust what we do not know, and this explains why the Christian faith affirms the primacy of the mind. As believers, our faith has intellectual content, so we need to be aware of certain facts such as sin, the resurrection, the atonement, the deity of Christ before we can receive salvation. It is easy to say that we love Jesus, but if we do not know these things about Him, then we cannot be saved. John 8:24 (ESV); "I told you that you would die in your sins, for unless you believe that I am He you will indeed die in your sins." Also, in Romans 10:9; "If you declare with your mouth, "Jesus is Lord," and believe in your heart that God raised him from the dead, you will be saved." God needs to go through the mind first before He can get to our hearts, and if we must love God rightly, then we must know some content. Simply knowing the facts is not sufficient; in fact, the Devil can write a better systematic theology than most saints but can never come to Jesus Christ because he does not like the things of God.

CHAPTER FOUR

A HEART THAT LOVES GOD

"*L*ove the Lord your God with all your heart and with all your soul and with all your mind and with all your strength. [a]" Mark 12:30

Our Lord and Savior Jesus Christ told us that we are to love God with the heart, soul, and body – our whole being. This commandment is undoubtedly a strong and mysterious one, take a look at 1 Peter 1:8; "Though you have not seen him, you love him; and even though you do not see him now, you believe in him and are filled with an inexpressible and glorious joy." Is it possible for us to love someone whom we have never seen before? How can we love God with our whole soul, our whole heart, our whole strength, and our whole mind? Do we have what it takes to love Him, as Christ said? Let's consider how to love God wholly and absolutely with our whole being.

It Starts with our Heart

In the Bible, the heart is more than just the seat of emotions; it is composed of our emotions, our will, mind as well as our conscience. It is the source of our thoughts, intentions, feelings and our sense of condemnation or guilt whenever we do something wrong. God created our hearts in a way that would enable us to love Him wholly and absolutely. But, in the world we live, our hearts love other things beside God, and we would find it hard to pray with the psalmist when he said in Psalm 73:25 (NIV); "Whom have I in heaven but you? And earth has nothing I desire besides you." As Christians, we must admit that we may love God to some extent, but He isn't our only or first love. The things of this world tug at our hearts daily. This makes it hard for us to obey the Lord's command about how we should love

God. 1 John 4:19-21 says, "We love because He first loved us. Whoever claims to love God yet hates a brother or sister is a liar." Although God commanded every one of us to love Him absolutely, it was never His intention that we develop the love for Him through our effort. God knows that we are not capable of such kind of love.

You need to understand that anytime God makes a demand, His intention is to help us meet the demand. The love we have for God actually originates from Him—from the love of God within us which is higher than any kind of love we can ever give. God sent His son Jesus Christ, and when we receive Jesus Christ as our Lord and Savior, we also receive all that Jesus is into our spirit. As believers, we can turn our hearts to Him where He is in our spirit, 2 Corinthians 3:16, 18; "But whenever anyone turns to the Lord, the veil is taken away."

There are several Bible verses that describe humans like mirrors that reflect what they behold. So, whenever our hearts are turned away from the Lord by things like preoccupation, sins, and love for worldly things, our hearts will be covered by a veil, and it becomes difficult for us to reflect the Lord. But, when we turn our hearts to the Lord within us, then the veil will be removed, and we can now see Christ. We can now behold His virtues, beauty, how wonderful He is, and He will impart what He is into us, and this includes His love.

Love Him with our Soul
Our soul – emotion, mind, and will – comprises a large part of our heart. One of the reasons why God created our soul is so that we could express Him. However, due to sin, we tend to express ourselves. We have our decisions, opinions, and feelings apart from God. When we turn our hearts to the Lord, then our love for Him grows. When we love Him with all our heart, then we also start loving Him with our soul. Our thoughts will align with God's thoughts, our decisions will align with His decision, and our feelings also will align with His feelings. As God continues to carry out His transforming work in us, we also begin to express and glorify Him.

With All our Mind
We need to love God with reason and intellect. Having faith does not imply that you should give up knowledge and understanding. To

love God with all your mind also has to do with study and thought that would help you grow your faith and enhance your relationship with God, Colossians 4:2; "Devote yourselves to prayer, being watchful and thankful." Isaiah 26:3; "You will keep in perfect peace those whose minds are steadfast because they trust in you." Ephesians 4:21-23; "When you heard about Christ and were taught in him in accordance with the truth that is in Jesus. You were taught, with regard to your former way of life, to put off your old self, which is being corrupted by its deceitful desires; to be made new in the attitude of your minds."

Loving God with All our Strength
Strength has to do with love in action. When we love God with all our strength, we love God with what we say and do. We honor Him with our resources, skills, abilities and actions, Philemon 1:6; "I pray that your partnership with us in the faith may be effective in deepening your understanding of every good thing we share for the sake of Christ."

How do you Love God?
First, you need to understand that if you feed your spirit with the Word of God, then your spirit will get stronger, and that's the starting point of how to love God. If you truly desire to love God more deeply, you have to modify your appetite and focus more on feeding your spirit with God's Word. Let's consider some ways to love God.

Always obey God's Word
"If you love me, keep my commands." John 14:15. In line with this Scripture, Jesus said that we should keep His commandments if we love Him, so obeying God is associated with loving Him. Devour the Word of God so that you can increase your love for God. On a daily basis, read the stories in the Bible and learn from the mistakes that others made. Study about our Savior, Jesus Christ; how He lived and the things He taught His followers. Reading the Bible helps us see how we should think, live and treat other people, so we apply Biblical principles to our lives. But when we read the Bible and ignore the things we read, then according to James, we only deceive ourselves. James 1:22-25; "Do not merely listen to the word, and so deceive yourselves. Do what it says. Anyone who listens to the word but does not do what it says is like someone who looks at his face in a mirror

and, after looking at himself, goes away and immediately forgets what he looks like. But whoever looks intently into the perfect law that gives freedom and continues in it—not forgetting what they have heard but doing it—they will be blessed in what they do."

Spend Quality Time in Prayers
All through the Gospels (Matthew, Mark, Luke, and John), we can clearly see several occasions where Christ left the people behind to pray. So, if the Son of God needed to spend time alone praying to the Father, then we also need the same. Actually, the lack of prayer is a sign of pride and unbelief. As believers, if we genuinely believe that when we pray, we will get answers to our prayers, then we would pray a lot more. When we fail to pray, then we are proudly implying that we are capable of handling things ourselves and there is no need to involve God.

Remember, prayer should not be fancy or complicated; it is simply communicating with God with an open heart and mind. Philippians 4:6-7; "Do not be anxious about anything, but in every situation, by prayer and petition, with thanksgiving, present your requests to God. And the peace of God, which transcends all understanding, will guard your hearts and your minds in Christ Jesus."

Always Forgive — No Exceptions
Although you may not like to hear this, it is the truth. Matthew 6:15; "But if you do not forgive others their sins, your Father will not forgive your sins." It is not possible as believers to receive what we are always unwilling to give, so you need to forgive others if you need forgiveness from God. Unforgiveness, as well as offenses, are all about the self. Whether people feel remorse for what they did or fail to apologize; whether we feel that they are taking advantage of us and hurting us; whether we feel that they don't really deserve to be forgiven, God still expects us to forgive. Every believer who genuinely wants to love God as Jesus instructed us must release everything they hold against anyone. The freedom that follows is indeed miraculous!

Avoid Worldly Mindsets
"Do not conform to the pattern of this world, but be transformed

by the renewing of your mind. Then you will be able to test and approve what God's will is—his good, pleasing and perfect will." Romans 12:2.

The ways of the world are contrary to God's ways. As believers that love God, we need to always evaluate our thoughts and mindsets. This will require us to compare them with God's Word, and any ideas or beliefs that we find to contradict the Bible must be rejected immediately. You need to be careful so that you do not participate in things that encourage worldly mindsets, thoughts, and opinions, Colossians 3:2; "Set your minds on things above, not on earthly things."

To love God more requires that you do your part by feeding and strengthening your spirit. This will require the study of the Bible and communicating with God on a regular basis.

A Heart That Loves God Loves Others
"Jesus replied: 'Love the Lord your God with all your heart and with all your soul and with all your mind.' This is the first and greatest commandment. 39 And the second is like it: 'Love your neighbor as yourself.'" Matthew 22:37-39.

"Do not seek revenge or bear a grudge against anyone among your people, but love your neighbor as yourself. I am the Lord." Leviticus 19:18.

Loving God more than others is the most loving thing that we can actually do for others. The reason is that when we love God most, then we will love others best. To an unbeliever, this sounds strange – how can you love people best by loving someone else? However, believers that have encountered Jesus Christ understand what this means.

The depth of love and grace that flows out from a believer toward other people is mainly based on them being filled with love for God; for all that He is for them and what He means to them in Jesus. Jesus gave the second commandment just like the first one which we read in the opening text for a reason. If we genuinely love God with all our heart, then we will definitely love our neighbor as ourselves. It is

43

similar to faith and works — when we truly have the first, then the second will naturally follow. If God is not the love of your life, then it is impossible to truly love our neighbors as ourselves.

One of the main reasons why we will love others best when we love God is that love in its purest and truest form can only come from God — God is love, 1 John 4:7-8; "Dear friends, let us love one another, for love comes from God. Everyone who loves has been born of God and knows God. Whoever does not love does not know God because God is love."

Love is a fundamental part of God's nature, and the reason why we can love God or anyone else is that God first loved us, 1 John 4:19; "We love because he first loved us." We can only freely give to other people what we have received from God. In Genesis 1:26, it is clear that we are God's image-bearers — designed to love God and our neighbors just as God loves God and others.

What Happens when We Fail to Love God the Most?
When we – or any other person or thing – become the ultimate love instead of God, then love will become diseased and distorted. This is a terrible thing, and it is the way the world loves; everyone loves in a way that seems right in their eyes. This also implies that everyone hates in whichever way they feel is not right in their eyes.

So, they turn out to be supreme "lovers of self," 2 Timothy 3:2; "People will be lovers of themselves, lovers of money, boastful, proud, abusive, disobedient to their parents, ungrateful, unholy," They also live in the passions of [their] flesh fulfilling the desires of their mind and body. In Ephesians 2:3, they are described as children deserving of wrath; "All of us also lived among them at one time, gratifying the cravings of our flesh and following its desires and thoughts. Like the rest, we were by nature deserving of wrath." This is a better explanation for the level of heartbreak, conflict, confusion, and violence in the world.

The most loving act that every believer should engage in is to love God most because when we do that, we will love others best. The way we love others reveals the extent of love we have for God, and this is why John puts it this way in 1 John 4:20; "Whoever claims to love God yet hates a brother or sister is a liar. For whoever does not love their brother and sister, whom they have seen, cannot love God, whom they have not seen."

CHAPTER FIVE

A CHEERFUL MERRY HEART

"**A** cheerful heart is good medicine, but a crushed spirit dries up the bones." Proverbs 17:22 In this section, we shall be taking a realistic look at what the Bible says about a merry heart. Let's start with Proverbs 12:25; "Anxiety weighs down the heart, but a kind word cheers it up." This passage implies that kind words are capable of cheering up people that are discouraged. Also, in Proverbs 14:10; "Each heart knows its own bitterness, and no one else can share its joy." We clearly see that the first part is true; each heart understands its own bitterness; most of us know our secret sorrows. Although some people may look well dressed, look good and have a radiant smile on their face, there is a story and a heartache behind that smile which we don't share.

In Proverbs 14:13; "Even in laughter the heart may ache, and rejoicing may end in grief." This is also another profound statement in the Bible. Even when we are putting up a brave face while facing the crowd, laughing in the midst of challenges, trying to be positive even when we are experiencing serious challenges deep within us – discouragement, heartache, turmoil, and despair. Seeing someone that is happy and smiling does not imply that everything is in order. Behind the laughter, there may be issues that you don't know about.

In Proverbs 14:30; "A heart at peace gives life to the body, but envy rots the bones." When you take a look at the word in Hebrew, it literally means that envy makes the bones disintegrate. This Bible passage talks about a kind of connection that exists between the physical and the spiritual. A kind of connection exists between body and heart, between the things that happen inside and what takes place outside. Our heart's attitude directly impacts the physical well-being or lack thereof. When your heart is at peace, it also gives life to your body, but envy causes the bones in your body to disintegrate.

Proverbs 15:13; "A happy heart makes the face cheerful, but heartache crushes the spirit." and 15:15; "All the days of the oppressed are wretched, but the cheerful heart has a continual feast." So, a cheerful heart will always eat a feast at the Lord's Table.

Now, let's take a look at Proverbs 17:22, the opening Bible verse for this chapter. The Bible makes it clear that a heart that is cheerful is a good medicine. To get a better translation, let's see how the King James Bible puts it: "A merry heart doeth good like medicine." This is a more interesting translation of the Hebrew. This Bible verse reveals to us that there is a relationship between our heart's condition and the condition of our body.

There is also a relationship between spiritual and physical health. When the Bible says that "A crushed spirit dries up the bones," it is literally saying that it sucks out the marrow of life from bones. Remember in Proverbs 18:1; "An unfriendly person pursues selfish ends and against all sound judgment starts quarrels." Most of us have seen people that struggle with weakness and sickness, but whenever you see them, they instantly cheer up. Even when they are down and out physically, they often make you happy anytime you see them simply because they have remained strong in spirit even though their body is wasting away.

On the flip side, we also know people around us that are sick but have a crushed spirit. After seeing them, you end up feeling worse than you felt when you came simply because they have ended up sucking all the life out of you too. Based on all these verses we have read, it is obvious that there is a strong relationship between your mental attitude and your physical well-being. In other words, what you are in your heart directly impacts your physical health. The things you have on the inside will eventually manifest themselves on the outside.

What's the Importance of a Merry Heart?
"And we know that in all things God works for the good of those

47

who love him, who[a] have been called according to his purpose." Romans 8:28. The world we live in is no doubt a difficult one; a world filled with heartache and despair, sickness and sin, but thanks to God sin is no longer the final word in this world. We have a word that is beyond the fall, beyond sin, beyond degradation, and that word is Jesus Christ. What the Bible says in Romans 8:28 is utterly inclusive – including everything that takes place in the life of a believer. It includes health, sickness, the good and bad, sunlight and shadow, wealth and poverty, life and death.

All these are things that can happen in the will of God to a believer. It means that no matter the outcome of the situation you are facing presently, whether life, death, good news or bad news, you must come to the knowledge that your trying moments are in God's hands. It forms a part of the "all things" that will definitely work together for good. One good example can be found in a letter that was written by former US President Reagan, which was printed in the Chicago Tribune: "I write because I do not want to keep a secret from the American people. My wife had breast cancer and we told you; they tried to assassinate me, and we told you; and now I have been diagnosed with Alzheimer's and I want to tell you. I want you to know this so that you will know about us and so that I can encourage other people whose families may be going through this disease. There is some stigma in some places attached to Alzheimer's. As for me, I feel very good right now, and as long as I am able, I will continue to do all the things I have been doing. I now begin the journey that will carry me into the sunset of life."

This is a remarkable phrase, and in its deepest sense, it is a Biblical phrase. In fact, at the end of his letter, President Reagan said: "Until the Lord calls me home, I intend to do what I have always done – to help people in whatever way I can." So, a merry heart is vital because God is telling us, "My children, there will be times when you will encounter certain things that you may not understand; sometimes, you may face heartache, pain, and hardship that is beyond what you feel you can endure. There will be times when you will almost wish that death could take you away from life, but I want to assure you that even in such situations, I am still with you and working out a plan in your life."

When we face difficult moments in our lives, what we need to do is to stand back and focus our minds on the fact that God is at work in our lives. Whether we feel it or not, whether we see it or not, whether we understand it or not and whether we believe it or not, God is at work. At such moments, our attitude makes a great difference. At such moments, it is most likely that you don't have an answer, but you must believe that there is a God that is at work in your situation. This is how you can have a merry heart even during the most challenging and darkest moments of your life.

You can have a cheerful spirit when you believe that there is a God in Heaven that not only loves you but is at work in ways that you can never see, believe or even understand. Another reason why a merry heart is important can be found in the opening text; "A merry heart doeth good like medicine." One of the tenses used in that verse is known as causative tense. Anytime you add a verb in the causative tense, you are trying to say that one thing will cause another thing to happen, and this is exactly what we see in the opening text. Let's take a look at a literal translation of the passage, "A heart that is cheerful causes good healing." This means that the Bible is telling us that your attitude – how you approach challenges and trials of life – will truly result in good healing, which is an amazing fact.

God desires that we have a merry heart; He provides the best for us in all aspects of life and in His Word, He has promised that he would supply all our needs, Philippians 4:19; "And my God will meet all your needs according to the riches of his glory in Christ Jesus."

He desires that we are full of joy, glad and merry; Psalm 68:3; "But may the righteous be glad and rejoice before God; may they be happy and joyful." In Hebrew, the word "be glad" means joyful and showing joy. Also, "merry" is translated from the same Hebrew word as "be glad," as in Psalm 68, while "medicine" is defined as a "cure" or healing. So, a glad heart makes the body healthy.

In the Biblical context, "heart" has to do with the seat of the personal life. People may not be able to determine our thoughts, but by looking at our faces, observing the things that we do and hearing the things we say, they may be able to read our thoughts. When you have

49

a merry heart, it will not just benefit you, but it will also benefit other people around you. When people discover that you have a merry heart — that you are joyful and glad — they may end up desiring to have what you have.

Cultivating a Merry Heart

This chapter would not be complete without having some tips on how to cultivate a merry heart. Before we look at the tips, you should understand that the starting point is to cultivate a relationship with God. Ensure that you spend time with the Lord. You shouldn't just seek peace with God, always bear in mind that we have peace with God through Jesus as is told in Romans 5:1; "Therefore, since we have been justified through faith, we have peace with God through our Lord Jesus Christ." Now, let's see other things you must do to cultivate a merry heart.

Develop a Forgiving Spirit

Ephesians 4:32; "Be kind and compassionate to one another, forgiving each other, just as in Christ God forgave you." Many people suffer physically simply because they harbor anger and bitterness and have refused to forgive those who hurt them. Are you wondering why people suffer deeply physically when they fail to forgive? Well, the answer is not difficult to find; envy rots the bones, anger rots bones, bitterness rots the bones, and unforgiveness rots the bones.

Do you often experience stomach aches, backaches, and headaches? Are you wondering why you are not doing well and are messed up most of the time? Are you wondering why you are unable to sleep at night? Why are you seeing an angry person whenever you stare at yourself in the mirror? Well, until you turn away from bitterness and anger, you will always be sick because the Bible says it will literally rot your bones.

One of the stories about forgiveness that seems almost impossible is the story in the Chicago Tribune with the headline "Pastor Forms a Bond With the Son's Killer." According to the story, the son of a pastor in Connecticut was murdered, but he became friends with the man that killed his son. Reverend Walter Everett forgave his son's killer and even assisted him in leaving prison early. It was recorded that he would officiate in the man's wedding. The pastor was quoted to have said, "I had known people whose loved ones had been murdered, and years afterward they still seemed consumed by the anger and hatred. I didn't want that to happen to me." The killer "Carlucci feels redeemed by the Pastor's compassion, but he could not understand how the pastor could ever forgive him. According to the killer, "He told me he had forgiven me for the love of God. Tears were coming down my face. It made me feel like I wanted to live, whereas before, I didn't care." As unbelievable as the story might seem, it is true, and it teaches that one must learn to forgive so that their bones don't rot.

Maintain a Long View of Life

Proverbs 15:15 says that a cheerful heart has a continual feast. Does this mean you will have a smooth and challenge-free life? The answer is definitely no. But what the Bible passage says implies that when you have a long view of life, when you take time to understand the fact that God is involved in all aspects of your life, including the unpleasant ones; when you have a broad view about the whole thing, then you can truly have a continual feast.

Embrace God's Word

"When your words came, I ate them; they were my joy and my heart's delight, for I bear your name, Lord God Almighty." Jeremiah 15:16. This Bible passage explains that the Word of God is what causes our heart to be merry. When we study God's word, we will learn about His heart for His Children. We need to fill our hearts with the truth in God's Word and believe what His Word says because God is able and willing to fulfill all that He has promised in His Word.

In spite of the challenges we are facing, we can still rejoice in knowing His promises, 3 John 2; "Dear friend, I pray that you may enjoy good health and that all may go well with you, even as your soul is getting along well." Also, we can rejoice because we can trust in Him, Psalm 5:11; "But let all who take refuge in you be glad; let them ever sing for joy. Spread your protection over them, that those who love your name may rejoice in you." Because we can pray to Him and have the hope that he will hear our prayer, 1 John 5:14-15; "This is the confidence we have in approaching God: that if we ask anything according to his will, he hears us. And if we know that he

51

hears us—whatever we ask—we know that we have what we asked of him." And because we can always call upon Him when we are in trouble and know that He will deliver us, Psalm 50:15; "And call on me in the day of trouble; I will deliver you, and you will honor me."

God's word gladdens our heart, and we need to read it on a daily basis; whether we read a chapter, a verse or more, all the time we spend in God's Word enables us to see why our hearts can be merry. We can rejoice in God's Word, knowing that He is capable of taking care of us regardless of the situation.

Learn to Dwell on Unseen Realities

There are many things that you believe to be true, but you cannot see them. For instance, think about eternity, the Holy Spirit, Heaven and the Lord Jesus Christ just as it was stated in Colossians 3:1-3; "Since, then, you have been raised with Christ, set your hearts on things above, where Christ is, seated at the right hand of God. Set your minds on things above, not on earthly things. For you died, and your life is now hidden with Christ in God."

Always Associate with People that are Cheerful

"Walk with the wise and become wise, for a companion of fools suffers harm." Proverbs 13:20. Some individuals are usually messed up not because of their circumstances but because they associate with people that are messed up already. When you hang around individuals that are always angry, you will most likely become angry. If you are bitter, you need to find out whether you are hanging around bitter people. If you are mad, it may be because you are always hanging around individuals that are angry and critical most of the time. Why don't you search for cheerful people and associate with them? This is one of the best ways to be cheerful and have a merry heart.

Don't be a Burden-Maker but a Load-Lifter

Galatians 6:2; "Carry each other's burdens, and in this way, you will fulfill the law of Christ." Avoid being one of those people that make life more difficult for others; instead, be a load lifter.

Learn to Live a Life of Active Love

Someone that is selfish can never be cheerful. Although they can be happy, they will never be cheerful. Only a lover, a giver, and someone that invests in the lives of other people can be cheerful. Only someone that is kind can really be cheerful and positive about life. So, start getting involved in other people's lives, and you will have a cheerful heart.

Control Your Thoughts

If we must have a merry heart, then we must have control over what we think of. As humans, there are several things that we cannot control, but God lovingly gave us the ability to control our thoughts. So, you can choose the kind of thoughts that you retain as well as the ones that you decide to discard.

One question that easily comes to your mind at this point is: "how can I control the thoughts that come to my mind?" Well, it is a moment-by-moment process to choose the thoughts that we retain and the ones we need to eliminate. One of the things that will help every believer do this is to keep learning and understanding the truths about the Word of God. We have the promises of God, and we can fill our hearts with such powerful promises in the Scripture — without leaving room for any negative thought to linger.

Take a look at Philippians 4:8; "Finally, brothers and sisters, whatever is true, whatever is noble, whatever is right, whatever is pure, whatever is lovely, whatever is admirable—if anything is excellent or praiseworthy—think about such things." While we continue to think about the positives of the Word of God, we will begin to incorporate His Word into the innermost part of our minds.

We will be able to fill our hearts with His Word and focus mainly on thinking about His Word and believe what His Word says concerning our lives and situation. Remember, what goes inside will manifest outside. We manifest physically in our lives the beliefs and ideas that we hold in our hearts, Proverbs 2:7 "He holds success in store for the upright, he is a shield to those whose walk is blameless."

When we have a merry heart, it positively affects our physical health, and it is joyfully expressed on our faces and opens doors for us to assist other people. As believers, our thoughts in our hearts greatly affect the things we say, our actions, and how other people see us. We can decide to have a merry heart daily by reading about the abundant promises that God has provided for every believer in His Word and trust that His word is true.

God has given us the power to change our thoughts, so we need to take one thought at a time and align it with what God says regarding us and also believe the Word of God. Since parents provide the needs of their children physically, spiritually and mentally, their children can live with joy in their hearts. In the same vein, since our heavenly father provides all the needs of His children, we can also have a merry heart!

CHAPTER SIX

HOW GOD GIVES US THE DESIRES OF OUR HEART

"*T*ake delight in the Lord, and he will give you the desires of your heart. Commit your way to the Lord; trust in him and he will do this" Psalm 37:4-5.

Is it really possible for God to grant the desires of our heart? Our actions demonstrate the level of trust we have in God. It's easy to believe what David said about God granting us the "desires of our heart" especially when things are going well. All of us have a desire; we hope to become, aspire to be, and strive to achieve something in our hearts.

An intense desire burns in our hearts for God to answer our prayer to be used by God for a special purpose. While some may desire that their spouse gets saved or experience the love that they once felt, others are praying for the return of a prodigal son. Each one of us has a deep heartfelt desire. What are your heart's desires? Do you want God to help you overcome an addiction? Is there a sin that you have not been able to overcome? Are you experiencing financial challenges or health issues? Is something missing in your life? Many believers have been able to receive the desires of their hearts, but how did they do it? How were they able to receive the answers to their prayers and fulfillment of their desires they have longed for? How do Christians receive the desires of their hearts? The answer to that question can be found in our opening text, Psalm 37:4.

Trust In God
If we genuinely trust in God, then we won't bother to seek solutions to things that bother us because The Word of God has answers to all our daily needs. In Psalm 37:3, David said, "Trust in

the Lord and do good; dwell in the land and enjoy safe pasture." If we trust in the Lord, then nothing in this world should trouble our hearts. If you don't trust in God, it will not be possible to please Him because you will fail to take Him at His Word, and He has promised that he would never forsake us in Hebrews 13:5, "Keep your lives free from the love of money and be content with what you have, because God has said, "Never will I leave you; never will I forsake you."

Learn to Delight in God
Any time children do the things that please their parents, we often get delighted. Children usually love helping out around the house even though it usually takes them much longer to accomplish something. But as believers, how does delighting in the Lord help us to receive the desires of our hearts? If we focus on always pleasing God in our lives, then we will be delighting the Lord, and this will reflect on the way we live our lives.

Remember, the Bible didn't say if God delights in us; rather, if we delight in Him. So, our side of the deal is to delight in the Lord, while God's part is to grant us the desires of our heart (whatever they may be) when we delight in Him. But anyone that delights in the Lord will have desires that align with pleasing God, which means that if you delight in the Lord, you won't need to desire evil things and expect God to grant you the desires of your heart.

Just imagine how God feels whenever believers delight in Him? See what Jesus said in John 14:15; "If you love me, keep my commands." If we truly love Him, then we will do what He says, and this explains why Jesus told His disciples; "And I will do whatever you ask in my name, so that the Father may be glorified in the Son. You may ask me for anything in my name, and I will do it," John 14:13-14. This does not imply that Jesus promised to do everything that we want but everything we need. He said; I will do it If only you will keep my commands. This is why we can ask "anything" in [His] name, but it has to be according to His will and not our will. Whatever we ask from God must align with His will and for His glory.

But how do you delight in the Lord? To answer this question, we need to first consider the meaning of delight and imagine that the focus and subject of your delight is God. Delight can be defined as a great satisfaction and joy; someone or something that gives great pleasure; to please and satisfy.

This is the key to discovering the desires of your heart. You need to take pleasure in God's goodness, rejoice in your salvation and allow Him to satisfy all your needs. In all that you do, learn to please Him, live contented with the things you already have because desires take time. This explains why the Bible in Psalm 37 clearly says wait, rest, trust and know. God delights in giving His people their heart's desires.

Delighting In God Ensures that Your Steps are Established

One of the benefits of delighting in the Lord is that God will establish your steps; Psalm 37:23; "The Lord makes firm the steps of the one who delights in him." Remember, delighting in someone implies that you have a heart that is focused on pleasing the person, listening to them and obeying them. So, delighting in the Lord means that even when you fall, God is there to uphold you as it is said in Psalm 37:24, "Though he may stumble, he will not fall, for the Lord upholds him with his hand." David clearly understands based on his experience that those who delight in God will be established, and this is what informed him to write in Psalm 37:25, "I was young and now I am old, yet I have never seen the righteous forsaken or their children begging bread."

After reading these precious promises in Scripture, you cannot but delight in God since you are assured that He will never forsake His own, Hebrews 13:5, "Keep your lives free from the love of money and be content with what you have, because God has said, "Never will I leave you; never will I forsake you."

Commit to God

According to the Psalmist in Psalm 37:5; "Commit your way to the Lord; trust in him, and he will do this." When you are committed to God, you will end up doing the things He says since you are His child. A child of God will definitely do what their father says, so when you commit to obedience, God will act. God does not act for people who do not obey Him. Obeying God pays, as in Psalm 37:6, "He will make your righteous reward shine like the dawn, your vindication like the noonday sun." This implies that when we are conscious that God will ensure justice is brought, we will easily commit to Him since we can trust Him to keep His promises.

Wait Upon the Lord

Waiting upon God may appear as a big waste of time; if you don't think the way God thinks, then waiting on Him will appear as a waste of time. But why do you need to wait on the Lord? The answer is in Psalm 37:9; "For those who are evil will be destroyed, but those who hope in the Lord will inherit the land." Christians must give God the chance to bring Justice in His timing. Although this might seem like a long wait, when you place the time against the backdrop of eternity, then it will be very short compared to the eternal glory that is coming. Romans 8:18, "I consider that our present sufferings are not worth comparing with the glory that will be revealed in us." This should increase our patience, and the Bible also admonishes us to "Refrain from anger and turn from wrath; do not fret—it leads only to evil," Psalm 37:8 God greatly delights in being kind and generous to His people, and He wants to provide us with the desires of our hearts. But the real question that you have to answer is; will you genuinely delight in Him? Are you prepared to trust Him to provide the best for you and all your needs rather than all your "greed?"

Consider God as your Father, which He is, and consider how you often please your earthly parents. What are the things that they take great delight in concerning you? In most cases, they are usually delighted when you do what they told you to do and whenever you behave the way they wanted you to. Now, you can also apply that same principle to delighting or pleasing the heart of your heavenly Father. If you genuinely delight in God, then rest assured that He will grant you the desires of your heart. As believers, when we genuinely delight in the Lord and abide in His presence, God's heart will start beating against ours. When we consistently and intimately do this, God will start infusing His ways as well as His desires into our hearts. This means that our desires will become God's desires; the one that delights in God will instinctively desire the things of God. When we are able to do this, God will begin to grant our heart's desires because God has sanctified it. For anything you are asking from God, you need to first draw intimately to His heart in worship and prayer, and He will grant your heart's desires.

It's possible that we may never receive the deepest and greatest desires of our hearts because God understands what is best for us. We might feel that what we desire is the best, but never forget that God knows the beginning to the end. Some of the things that we desire greatly may not be God's purpose for our lives.

CHAPTER SEVEN

GUARDING THE HEART

"Above all else, guard your heart, for everything you do flows from it. Keep your mouth free of perversity; keep corrupt talk far from your lips. Let your eyes look straight ahead; fix your gaze directly before you. Give careful thought to the paths for your feet and be steadfast in all your ways. Do not turn to the right or the left; keep your foot from evil." Proverbs 4:23-27

The book of Proverbs clearly interweaves practical matters with spiritual matters and makes life the beautiful thing that God intends it to be. Any believer that knows God and is right with God will definitely live an intensely practical, perfectly natural, and deeply spiritual life all at the same time, just as God intends. In the Old Testament, we find that the word "heart" was used more than 800 times, but over 200 times, it deals with the emotions, the thought of life, the wellsprings of life as well as the things that mold and motivate us.

What the Bible refers to as the heart can also be regarded as the thought life. But why is the heart so vital? Why did Solomon admonish his son that "above all else, guard your heart; for out of it are the issues of life?" The reason is that the heart or thought life controls the rest of your life.

Just tell me about what you think, and I'll let you know who you are and the life you live. You must understand that what you think is what you are — your thoughts control you — Proverbs 23:7; "for he is the kind of person who is always thinking about the cost. "Eat and drink," he says to you, but his heart is not with you." The KJV Bible says, "As a man thinketh in his heart, so is he." Know that your thoughts — negative, positive, good or bad — control how you be have. How you behave makes for your attitude and your attitude is the sum of all your thoughts. Your attitude actually leads to your actions.

The Meaning of Guard Sometimes, the word "guard" as clearly written in Proverbs 4:23, could be regarded as seal, bar or coat in a shield of lead. But in Hebrew, the word "keep" (which is interchangeable with guard) literally implies "to set a watchman over your heart." The Bible does not imply in this passage that we should guard our hearts with our own strength; instead, what God wants is for believers to guard their hearts by filtering their thoughts, desires, emotions, and responses through the Word of God.

God is the primary watchman that protects our soul, and His primary means of defense is the sword of the Scripture. So, we need to keep ourselves in God's Word, let His Word fill our hearts or thoughts, and He will keep our hearts. Psalm 18:30, "As for God, his way is perfect: The Lord's word is flawless; he shields all who take refuge in him." Also, take a look at Psalm 119:9, "How can a young person stay on the path of purity? By living according to your word." Proverbs 2:7-8, "He holds success in store for the upright, he is a shield to those whose walk is blameless, for he guards the course of the just and protects the way of his faithful ones."

Your Actions are Controlled by Your Thoughts
Every good psychologist will always explain this fact to you
"Sow a thought, reap a deed. Sow a deed, reap a habit. Sow a habit, reap a character. Sow a character, reap a destiny." Stephen Covey

Before doing anything, you must think about it. Your thoughts lead to attitudes, and your attitudes lead to actions which, in turn, lead to achievements. Everything starts with the thought of life. All your achievements will be a result of all your thoughts. The importance of the heart explains why God in the Old Testament destroyed an entire civilization simply because their "heart was faulty." Genesis 6:5, "The Lord saw how great the wickedness of the human race had become on the earth, and that every inclination of the thoughts of the human heart was only evil all the time."

God declared that the thoughts of their hearts are so evil that He had to destroy them. This caused Him to send the flood to wipe them out from the face of the earth. The core problem of humans is the problem of the human heart, and we still face the same problem that the people God destroyed faced — the heart problem.

Why the Heart Needs Guarding

There are several reasons why you need to guard your heart. Guard your heart because it is extremely valuable. We don't bother guarding things that are worthless; for instance, you can easily take out your garbage to the street every week, and it will be picked up maybe the next morning. For as long as it sits on the sidewalk all through the night, it is totally unguarded. But have you ever cared to ask why the garbage is unguarded? Well, the answer is not difficult — it's completely worthless. But this is not the case with your heart because it is the essence of who you are. Your heart can be regarded as your authentic self - the very core of your being. It is where your desires, dreams, and passions live and the part of you that connects with God and the people around you.

Another reason why the heart needs guarding is that it is desperately sick; in fact, it is incurably wicked, Jeremiah 17:9b, "The heart is deceitful above all things and beyond cure. Who can understand it?" Don't forget that the word "heart" may be regarded as emotions, the mind, the inner man or the will. Because the sinful nature cannot be eliminated, it can only be changed for the better. Human reformation is not capable of working on the heart of man, and this is why anyone that trusts in his or her own heart is a fool. We must not submit to the pull of the old nature which is there to deceive every believer.

It is the source of all the things you do: In the words of King Solomon, your heart is the "wellspring of life." This implies your heart is the source of other things in your life. When the source of a spring is poisoned, the flow will become toxic, and if you decide to stop the spring, then you will stop the flow of water. In both cases, you will threaten the life downstream — the plants, animals, and humans that depend on the spring. This is similar to your heart; if your heart is unhealthy, it will impact every other aspect of your life;

it will threaten your friends, your career, your family, your legacy and your ministry. So, you must guard your heart. The heart is not just deceitful, but more deceitful than anything else; Jeremiah 17:9. Because of the natural self-centeredness, self-protective ways, devices and selfishness of the heart, we cannot trust it (Psalm 81:12-14; Jer. 17:9; 2:13).

Our hearts are constantly being attacked. Another important reason why you need to guard your heart is that as believers, we are living in a combat zone — one with casualties. Many Christians are not conscious of this raging war. As Christians, we have an enemy that is determined to destroy us. Apart from the fact that the devil opposes God, he also opposes all the things that are aligned with God, and this includes every believer.

How Can You Guard Your Heart?
"Do not conform to the pattern of this world, but be transformed by the renewing of your mind. Then you will be able to test and approve what God's will is—his good, pleasing and perfect will." Romans 12:2.

How does God change the life of a person? God simply changes your thought process when he changes how you think. What Solomon was telling His son in the opening text was, "Son, protect, guard and be careful about your thought life. The Lord Jesus wants us as believers to present our bodies to Him — and this includes our mind — that He might transform us."

This explains why the devil fights to have control of our mind. You must understand how important it is for us as Christians to keep our hearts because there is a fierce battle for the control of our minds. When you have God in your heart, then you will think right, do right and live right, but when God is not in your heart, you will think wrongly, do wrong and live wrongly. You must be careful what comes into your heart and endeavor to think pure thoughts.

Remember, a text that lacks context is a pretext, so context is essential. In the opening passage, we can see that Solomon was talking about the sexual affairs of a young man. So, he was warning his son about having impure and immoral thoughts in his heart and life. It is quite interesting to note that God created us in a way that prevents us from thinking two things simultaneously.

So, as a Christian, how do you avoid thinking about what is wrong? Focus your thoughts on what is right, and as long as you think what is right, you can never think what is wrong. Put differently, simply fill yourself with God's Word; fill your heart with the Word of God! Psalm 119:9-11, "How can a young person stay on the path of purity? By living according to your word. I seek you with all my heart; do not let me stray from your commands. I have hidden your word in my heart that I might not sin against you."

Fill up your Heart with God's Word
In our daily lives, we often face several distractions that tend to occupy our minds. So, how can we think pure thoughts amid ungodly information and images that we are often exposed to? It is not by thinking about trees, birds, and flowers; it is by thinking positive thoughts, by focusing on the Word of God. Hebrews 4:12, "For the word of God is alive and active. Sharper than any double-edged sword, it penetrates even to the dividing of soul and spirit, joints and marrow; it judges the thoughts and attitudes of the heart."

God intends to minister to you from your thought life as well as through your thought life. You must understand that a God-controlled thought life will:

- Guard your sight; Proverbs 4:25
- Govern what you say; Proverbs 4:24 and
- Guide your steps; Proverbs 4:27

How do you determine what you have in your heart? It is by listening to the things that come out of your mouth; remember, Jesus said in Matthew 12:34, "You brood of vipers, how can you who are evil say anything good? For the mouth speaks what the heart is full of."

When you have a clear mind and one that is right with God; when the thoughts you think are thoughts of Christ and when you are transformed by God's Word and the power of the Holy Spirit in your thought life, then you will definitely do God's will.

Always Protect What Comes in
Everything we encounter in life is competing for our resources, time and money. In fact, when you turn on the television or go out to work or to take a walk, you will encounter several things that are demanding your attention: language, money, sex, music, videos, pride, books, power, etc. You must be careful of the things that you allow into your heart. Guard the things that influence you, the things you listen and watch.

Discipline your eyes to look away from lust and, instead of folly, listen to wisdom — the Word of God. You have to guard your heart against harm and a culture that is anti-God. Replace them with godly thoughts, and your heart will remain protected.

What is God leading you to do?
Each one of us has different skills and desires, and it's a good thing. God intentionally made every one of us different and also calls us to follow Him in different ways. While some believers will be stay-at-home moms, others may become pastors, musicians, writers, teachers, EMTs, mechanics, etc. So, what is God asking you to do? What are the things that you desire and can't stop thinking about, and how do you really serve God with your desire? It's most likely that God is leading you to do that which you are unable to stop thinking about, so go ahead and do what God is calling you to do. The longer you wait to quench the desire of your heart, the more you will strain it.

CHAPTER EIGHT

TRUSTING THE LORD WITH OUR WHOLE HEART

"*T*rust in the Lord with all your heart and lean not on your own understanding." Proverbs 3:5

Learning and education have in some ways become idols that people are increasingly bowing to - a time of exceeding pride in human knowledge as well as accomplishment. The level of information that humanity has acquired is beyond what an individual can comprehend fully, and it is available. The culture we live in greatly considers the rights and desires of every person as the greatest good. In this culture, you can have anything that you want or become anything that you want provided that it does not cause any harm to other people or prevent them from their desires.

However, as Christians, in these times, it is essential for us to always have constant reminders of what it truly means to put our trust only in the Lord God Almighty. So, what does it mean to trust the Lord with your whole heart?

It Means Placing Your Confidence in God Alone
Just as the opening scripture clearly states, trusting in the Lord is beyond believing who he is and the things he says. It has to do with trust, and trust here implies "to have confidence in," and having confidence in something means that you have an assurance that leads to action. Having your trust in the Lord is a faith that can allow you to serve boldly, and you have to allow this confidence to infuse your whole being.

You must ensure that all your knowledge, will and wisdom should be saturated in action — producing assurance of God. Anytime you lean on your own understanding, you are actually trusting your knowledge as well as discernment to support you through life. But remember in Jeremiah 17:9, which reveals to us the problem with trusting our heart — because it is deceitful above all things and desperately sick, who can understand it?

You can never depend on your sinful nature. One way you can cultivate a God-trusting heart is to meditate on Scripture, companionship with believers, and spend time in prayer. These are the things that tune your hearts to the Holy Spirit that dwells in us, and this causes us to rely less on ourselves and rely more on God. It helps us to serve God in good times and bad, in health and sickness, in the battle of sin and peace of His rest.

Trusting God also Implies Acknowledging Him in Everything
"In all your ways, submit to him, and he will make your paths straight." Proverbs 3:6

To always acknowledge God means knowing God wherever we are and in whatever we do. It is not just intellectual assent; rather, it should be an act of perceiving God's character and will in every moment of your life. If we actually dedicate ourselves to seeking and trusting in God in every circumstance, are we then going to believe that life will be very easy and we will not encounter any trouble?

Each of us has experienced life enough to know that it is not the case. Rather, we should expect that our journey in life will definitely lead to Him, and we will not be moved when we encounter trials. Take a look at Jeremiah 17:7-8, "But blessed is the one who trusts in the Lord, whose confidence is in him. They will be like a tree planted by the water that sends out its roots by the stream. It does not fear when heat comes; its leaves are always green. It has no worries in a year of drought and never fails to bear fruit."

It does not imply that life would not have difficulties. Instead, it means that those difficulties are nothing that we should fear. We should be confident in God despite the difficulties, and He will keep us useful and vibrant to His will even when we feel that the times are against us. When we continue to trust God more and have the confidence to act based on His will, God may deprive us of opportunities that may appear great simply because He has called us to do something else.

When you acknowledge God in everything, it means that we are conscious that no circumstance comes to us outside the will of God. This knowledge will give us the strength to overcome pains, difficulties, and fears because we are conscious of the fact that God will always be by our side.

Trusting God Means to Fear God

"Do not be wise in your own eyes; fear the Lord and shun evil." Proverbs 3:7. Placing our trust in Man's wisdom or looking up to our skills and abilities — both individually and corporately — is futile in the extreme. Remember in 1 Corinthians 3:19-21, "For the wisdom of this world is foolishness in God's sight. As it is written: "He catches the wise in their craftiness"; and again, "The Lord knows that the thoughts of the wise are futile." 21 So then, no more boasting about human leaders! All things are yours."

Regardless of what we think we know, God knows more, and He is more capable of ridiculing our supposed wisdom and using it for His greater purpose. You have to learn to trust the wisdom of God instead of your own, and what will prevent you from being enamored by your knowledge is to fear God. The best solution to "being wise in [our] own eyes" is to respectfully fear Him and stand in awe of the Lord. God greatly frowns at sin, and being conscious of how sublime and fearsome God is, will serve as a cure for us being enamored by our knowledge. The fear of God helps us to stay away from evil in any form, and it also makes His loving kindness more incredible.

Trusting in God is indeed the only path to life, and this can be seen clearly in the life and work of Jesus Christ. He fully trusted the Father in His life even to His death — His work on the cross, His resurrection, and ascension. He offers everyone that believes in Him new life and pours out the Holy Spirit into our hearts. In a world of misplaced trusts, damaged lives and broken promises, Jesus is the only unshakable, unbreakable and unchangeable God that is worthy of all our trust. Jesus trusted the Father totally with all His heart, and He made a path for our salvation so that we can also trust Him. Now that we know what it means to trust in the Lord, with all our heart, how can we trust Him?

How to Trust the Lord with All Your Heart Never Depend on Yourself

In the world we live in, trust is something that must be earned, but it seems to be in short supply. However, Solomon knew that trusting in the Lord is where we need to start from when he wrote Proverbs 3:5. As Christians, we have faced challenges and disappointments that taught us to only depend on ourselves. However, if we must live the kind of life that God called us to, then we must unlearn that lesson and rest in God's understanding. There is no doubt that God possesses all wisdom, as stated in Romans 11:33, "Oh, the depth of the riches and wisdom and knowledge of God! How unsearchable his judgments, and his paths beyond tracing out!"

Although it can be a tough experience to trust God completely, we need to consciously lay aside our expectations, goals, and plans each day and surrender to God's plans for us.

If you Don't Feel Like Trusting God Absolutely, Cry out to Him

There are times when we don't feel like trusting God the way we ought to, but remember that surrendering to God starts with our lips as well as thoughts. What we need to depend on God exceeds commitment; we also need to cry out to God to express our dependence on Him as it is said in Proverbs 3:6.

Whenever we pray, we admit that God's ways are higher than our ways, and we are also dropping all our burdens and dreams in God's capable hands. Scripture promises that when we reach out to God in prayer, He hears us; Psalm 55:17, "Evening morning and noon I cry out in distress, and he hears my voice." We have already given God the keys to our lives, and we are confident that He is able to lead us.

Stay Away from Evil

Our relationship with God can easily get cluttered by so many worldly things. This is what John described as the desires of the flesh, the pride in our lives and the lust of the eyes, 1 John 2:16; "For everything in the world-the lust of the flesh, the lust of the eyes, and the pride of life—comes not from the Father but from the world." So, our blessing can turn into stumbling blocks anytime we think that we deserve them or feel that we need them to be happy. Life works best when we remember that God is the true source of all our blessings and learn to focus on the things that please Him, as explained in Proverbs 3:7.

Sometimes, separating ourselves from bad influences that continuously drag us down is the only way to live the life that God wants us to live, II Timothy 2:22; "Flee the evil desires of youth and pursue righteousness, faith, love and peace, along with those who call on the Lord out of a pure heart."

How do you flee from evil desires that often pull at you? It is by spending quality time crying to God and leaning on Him. When we shun evil, then God has promised to honor our commitment, Proverbs 3:8, "This will bring health to your body and nourishment to your bones." We will find abundant life when we pursue Him and run away from the evil which does not often come naturally to most Christians. But we need to make a serious change.

Learn to Put God First

Putting ourselves first is very easy to do. We want to congratulate ourselves with a reward when something good happens. But, when something bad happens, we either find someone else to blame or console ourselves. So, we usually focus on ourselves mainly. This struggle is even harder when it has to do with money. Solomon understood that even all the money he had does not belong to him, and that is why he admonishes us in Proverbs 3:9-10, "Honor the Lord with your wealth, with the first fruits of all your crops; then your barns will be filled to overflowing, and your vats will brim over with new wine."

For instance, when we hand the first part of our paycheck to God, it requires a lot of faith, but it means that we are focused on God.

Learn to Listen to the Holy Spirit

While Jesus Christ was about to leave, He promised His disciples that He would send the Holy Spirit to the Church and informed His disciples that the Spirit of God who is our counselor would serve as our spiritual compass. Take a look at John 14:26, "But the Advocate, the Holy Spirit, whom the Father will send in my name, will teach you all things and will remind you of everything I have said to you."

The Holy Spirit guides us as we go through our day, so we don't have to worry about getting things right or doing it alone because the Spirit of God will lead us into all truth and also protect us. II Timothy 1:14 states, "Guard the good deposit that was entrusted to you—guard it with the help of the Holy Spirit who lives in us."

CHAPTER NINE

THE THOUGHTS OF YOUR HEART

"*F*or he is the kind of person who is always thinking about the cost. "Eat and drink," he says to you, but his heart is not with you." Proverbs 23:7.

During the process of sanctification, one of the things that the Lord will do is to help you with the right thinking in your mind as well as your thought process. The things you chose to think of and dwell on will either make or break you as to the kind of person you will become in life. Take a look at the opening text from Scripture. You will notice the keyword there, which is "thinks." The word "thinks" informs you that God is focused on your thought processes, that is, what you think about each day.

We can interpret Proverbs 23:7 as "You can become what you think." Yes, you are what you think, and you can easily see this principle in our world today. It is not hard to identify those who act on this principle, the way which the Lord has intended for every believer, and those who act to the contrary. Those who seem happier and fulfilled with their lives have a sound mind and have the right or positive thoughts in their lives. They decide to focus on the more positive side of life instead of thinking and dwelling on the negative side of life.

Those that are unhappy and unfulfilled are the ones that are always depressed and pessimistic all the time. They have a negative attitude toward anything and anybody. Although we live in a cursed and fallen world that has a mixture of life and death, our Lord Jesus Christ told us that we would experience different kinds of trials and tribulations in life from time to time.

Life has two sides; one side is the darker side of life while the second side is the brighter, good and positive side of life. So, life is not always about doom, death, and destruction. Even in worst-case scenarios, there will always be light at the end of the storm. Remember, every Christian has God on their side to assist them in overcoming the storms of life. Those whose thoughts are positive and happy have chosen to focus on the brighter side of life regardless of the situation they may find themselves in.

Pessimistic people have chosen to dwell on all the bad and terrible things in life. No matter how good they experience in life, they will always feel that something much better could have come their way. Because of the negative and morbid thoughts in their heart, nothing really makes them happy, and they are never content because nothing good is ever sufficient for them.

As Christians, we have been clearly instructed that we are free to choose the kind of thoughts in our hearts. We don't have to be slaves to pessimistic and negative thoughts. We can consciously choose what we think about. The thoughts of our heart or our thinking process do not control us; instead, we control them.

Dealing with Negative Thoughts
If you discover that you are having negative thoughts, then know that they can be broken. Negative thinking has actually become a mental stronghold since it drags people down into dwelling on negative thoughts for a long period. However, according to Scripture, it is possible for believers to take "captive" the things they think about. This implies that as Christians, we are directly responsible for the things we think about and dwell on to ensure that the thoughts of our heart align with God's Word and how God wants us to think about things.

The power to choose our thoughts lies with us! You cannot blame God or anyone else if you choose to dwell constantly on the negative and darker side of your own free will. You need to learn how to develop the right thinking in your thought process. Although our part as believers is to endeavor to think and dwell on things that our God wants us to focus on, it is obvious that most of us have a limited mental and psychological strength in this area.

Some people actually do better than others in dealing with negative thoughts, and this is where the help of the Spirit of God is greatly needed. The Holy Spirit will help your thought process. He will straighten and establish your thoughts in the Lord just the way God wants it to be. It is part of the sanctification process that every Christian experiences which cannot be achieved in one day. Remember, you might have been dwelling in negative mindsets for a very long time, and the process of modifying them is gradual and progressive.

Your role during this sanctification process is to work closely with the Spirit of God when He starts sanctifying you. The Spirit of God will target specific areas in your thoughts where you are completely off base. If the Spirit of God tells you that you should not be too judgmental or critical of other people, for instance, then it is your part to do your best to cast down such negative and destructive thoughts in your heart and replace them with godly and positive thoughts.

This process is often a difficult one for some people because they will be forced to admit their character flaws as well as imperfections that have to be dealt with in their mind, soul, and personality. The Holy Spirit will never force the changes on you. Instead, He will inform you of what He wants to remove from your system and the things he wants to add. When you choose to work with Him on some of these changes, God will enable the supernatural power of the Holy Spirit to begin the transformation process and sanctify you in ways that please Him the most.

Being Transformed by the Renewing of Your Mind
"Therefore, I urge you, brothers and sisters, in view of God's mercy, to offer your bodies as a living sacrifice, holy and pleasing to God—this is your true and proper worship." Romans 12:1.

Remember, part of your mind is your thought process, that is, the things you choose to think about and dwell on. Just as the Biblical text says, part of the transformation and sanctification process with the Holy Spirit involves the renewal of your mind through God's Word and by the Spirit of God. Ephesians 4:22-24, "You were taught, with regard to your former way of life, to put off your old self, which is being corrupted by its deceitful desires; to be made new in the attitude of your minds; and to put on the new self, created to be like God in true righteousness and holiness."

Your inner man and will can be renewed on a daily and progressive basis. 2 Corinthians 4:16, "Therefore, we do not lose heart. Though outwardly we are wasting away, yet inwardly, we are being renewed day by day."

When God mentions that our inner spiritual transformation is accomplished by getting our minds properly renewed in Him, He is actually revealing a powerful, incredible, spiritual secret that is also a part of the sanctification process.

Now We Have the Mind of Christ
"Who has known the mind of the Lord so as to instruct him?" But we have the mind of Christ." 1 Corinthians 2:16.

Scripture tells us that we have the "mind of Christ." Consider the ramifications, implications, and power of this statement. Since we have the Spirit of God dwelling in us, we now have direct access to God and Jesus Christ who lives in heaven. Because we have this direct access to Jesus through the Spirit of God, we now have the mind of Christ operating through us.

Jesus Christ, through the Spirit of God, can now begin to impart His thoughts as well as His ways of thinking directly into the minds of every Christian. The direct transmission of His thoughts to us through the Spirit of God is so perfect, clear and powerful that Scripture declares that we now have the mind of Christ. So, we now have the power of the Holy Spirit operating in us to assist us in getting our thought life cleaned up and also the power of Jesus Christ available to us since he will grant us access to His own mind to enable us to learn how we should think and act in life.

75

In 1 Corinthians 11:1, the Bible admonishes us to imitate Christ — act just like Christ wants us to. The two Bible readings are like two pieces of a jigsaw puzzle — Jesus wants us to think the way He thinks and also act like Him. Jesus now becomes the perfect role model that we can now pattern our inner as well as outer life.

We have Been Given a Sound Mind
"For the Spirit God gave us does not make us timid but gives us power, love, and self-discipline." 2 Timothy 1:7

The word self-discipline is used in the NIV Bible, while "sound mind" is used in the KJV Bible. In times like the one we live in now, this Scripture is a powerful and important one. Take a look around you, and you will discover that many carnal Christians, as well as nonbelievers, are not acting on a very sound mind. Just spend five to ten minutes with some people, and you can easily tell those that are acting with a sound mind and those that are not.

The sexual and material lust of this world is so alarming and overwhelming for some of these individuals that all that they have their minds constantly focused on is trying to acquire money, power and enjoy sex as much as they possibly can. Because of this type of lustful pursuits, the thoughts of their hearts have completely become distorted, debased, warped and downright unstable.

We have seen most marriages and good relationships broken up because people's minds have become unsound due to the deterioration and corruption that will happen in their minds when they go after these lustful and material pursuits for a long time. Because of the deterioration in the minds of people, marriages have been lost, good relationships have been lost, and some have deteriorated to the extent of taking their life.

You must realize that one of the most amazing gifts that every Christian can ever enjoy, especially in the kind of world we live in today, is being blessed with a clear, good and sound mind in the Lord. With all the crazy information and things that we encounter in life, you need to really hold on to the Word of God. Regardless of the severity of the storm you may have to deal with in life, you must understand that you have the mind of Christ now as well as the power of the Spirit of God operating through you to enable you to harbor powerful and sound thoughts in your heart.

The Lord will Establish Your Thoughts

"Commit to the Lord whatever you do, and he will establish your plans." Proverbs 16:3

You must understand that God is all-knowing and all-powerful, and this means that He has direct access into your thought life. Other people, as well as Demons, cannot read your mind or thoughts. It is your private area, but since God is able to read your thoughts, you can never hide anything from Him. Most people love hiding things from people close to them, but they can never fool God because He is always one step ahead of us — even in our personal and private thought life as well as the things you choose to think about and dwell on.

According to the Bible, the thoughts of the wicked are an abomination to the Lord as Proverbs 15:26 says, "The Lord detests the thoughts of the wicked, but gracious words are pure in his sight." God used an intense word when describing people's thoughts that are regarded as very wicked and evil; He used "abomination" in KJV while "detest" is used in the NIV Bible. All around us, we see and hear news of people who have carried out horrific crimes that depict the extent of the wickedness of people's thoughts. God is always watching the thought life of every one of us, and as believers, we need to endeavor to clean it up.

The opening text also explains that if we commit our works to the Lord, then we have fully surrendered to Him and when we operate in full surrender to Him, then the Spirit of God can start working in us to help us solidify our thought life.

Christians should Bring All Thoughts into
Captivity to the Obedience of Christ

As Christians, how do we handle the thoughts in our hearts? Well, that is what this Bible verse tells us, 2 Corinthians 10:3-5, "For though we live in the world, we do not wage war as the world does.

The weapons we fight with are not the weapons of the world. On the contrary, they have divine power to demolish strongholds. We demolish arguments and every pretension that sets itself up against the knowledge of God, and we take captive every thought to make it obedient to Christ."

God is telling us to bring every thought into captivity to the obedience of Christ. This implies that we are directly responsible for the things we decide to think about and dwell on. It is our duty to bring every thought into "captivity" to Christ and not to others, including parents, friends, or even hypnotists who attempt to plant suggestions into people's minds. God made use of the word "captivity" in the opening text mainly to tell us that it is our duty to make some kind of concerted effort on our end to properly control our thought life and prevent it from getting out of control, especially when it comes to bad and carnal kinds of thoughts.

We are expected to take hold of our thoughts and ensure that what we think and our thoughts align with how God would like us to think about things. It is a tall order for many of us to maintain proper control of all kinds of bad thoughts that we encounter every day, but this is where the Spirit of God comes in to help us. To make it happen, we must be ready to allow Him to put us through the sanctification process.

It is our duty to do our best to control our thought life, but when we get to the point where we fail or end up in areas where we find it hard to conquer with our willpower, then the Holy Spirit will step in and supernaturally provide His help and strength to help you overcome such difficult hurdles.

Remember, it is impossible for you not to experience bad thoughts at some point in life that will get you into trouble with the Lord, but what you decide to do with such thoughts when they cross your mind is what matters most. You have two main choices; either decide to allow the bad thought to get out of your mind and refuse to give it another thought, or you can decide to start thinking about the bad thoughts and dwell on them. If you decide to think and dwell on the bad thoughts, you will begin to feed them, and as soon as you begin to feed them, they will start growing. When it starts growing, then it will culminate into a mental stronghold that you will find hard to eradicate from your thought process. When the mental stronghold continues to grow deeper and stronger, then you will start getting the actual desire to act on the thoughts. As soon as you start acting on it, you will start forming an actual addiction which will cause you to repeat the same behavior several times.

At this point, you will require the supernatural power of the Holy Spirit to help set you free from addictive and compulsive behavior. Consider this: all this actually started with just one simple and little thought that crossed your mind, which you nurtured by thinking and dwelling on it. This is actually how most addictions are formed, especially the more aberrant types like pedophiles. Always be conscious of what the Bible says on a daily basis as you consciously guard your heart; "For as he thinks in his heart, so is he."

CHAPTER TEN

GOD'S WORD IN OUR HEARTS

"*B*lessed are those whose ways are blameless, who walk according to the law of the Lord. Blessed are those who keep his statutes and seek him with all their heart—they do no wrong but follow his ways." Psalm 119:1-3

The duty of every Christian is to hide the Word of God in their hearts. Doing this corresponds to a right end, and their knowledge and delight in it has to be directed in practice. Hiding God's Word in their hearts is one of the essential duties and practices of Christians. This is confirmed in Joshua 1:8, "Keep this Book of the Law always on your lips; meditate on it day and night, so that you may be careful to do everything written in it. Then you will be prosperous and successful." And you can also find it in Job 22:22, "Accept instruction from his mouth and lay up his words in your heart."

So, as a believer, you need to lay up God's Word just like you would also do precious things so that they don't get lost. You need to lay them up just like a treasure that you can use on all occasions. Let these words not be in your memory alone, but also allow the affections to be moved therewith; Colossians 3:16, "Let the message of Christ dwell among you richly as you teach and admonish one another with all wisdom through psalms, hymns, and songs from the Spirit, singing to God with gratitude in your hearts." You need to be very diligent in studying God's Word so that it will become familiar to you. You can achieve this by constantly hearing, reading, meditating and also conferring about it. Do not allow God's word to stand at the door like a stranger. Instead, give it access into the inner room and familiarize yourself with it.

What does it Mean to Hide God's Word in Our Hearts?
When we are told to hide His Word in our hearts, it means:

• Understanding His Word and having a competent knowledge of it. The way we take things into our soul is by understanding.Proverbs 2:10 says, "For wisdom will enter your heart, and knowledge will be pleasant to your soul."

• It also means we assent to it by faith. God's Word is settled in our hearts by faith. Else, it would vanish as clearly explained in Hebrews 4:2, "For we also have had the good news proclaimed to us, just as they did; but the message they heard was of no value to them, because they did not share the faith of those who obeyed."

Hiding God's Word in our heart implies that it should be kindly entertained. John 8:37 states, "I know that you are Abraham's descendants. Yet you are looking for a way to kill me because you have no room for my word."

Today, people are easily possessed with prejudice and lust that they leave no room at all for God's Word. Although the Word enters their hearts with evidence and power, they fail to entertain it there. Instead, they cast it out just like they would cast out a stranger or an unwelcome guest.

Hiding God's word is when it is deeply rooted in us. Many believers experience flashes for a time. Their affections may actually be aloft, and they experience outstanding elevations of joy, but lack sound grace. John 5:35 says, "John was a lamp that burned and gave light, and you chose for a time to enjoy his light." God's Word needs to be appreciated and loved if we would profit from it and have comfort. In vain do believers expect fruit until the engrafted Word of God is rooted in them. James 1:21, "Therefore, get rid of all moral filth and the evil that is so prevalent and humbly accept the word planted in you, which can save you."

Why We Need to Hide God's Word in Our Hearts
As Christians, there are several reasons why we must hide the Word of God in our hearts, such as follows:

1. So it Would be Ready for Our Use

This is the first main reason why we need to hide the Word in our hearts. As humans, we lay up principles in our hearts that we will apply when faced with several life circumstances. When you hide the Word in your heart, it will be prepared to break out in practice and help you direct your ways while carrying out your daily tasks. For instance, if you decide to go to the market whenever you need to purchase anything you want to use, it makes you a poor housekeeper. But a better way to handle such affairs is to purchase the things you know you will need on other days, so you don't have to visit the market whenever you need them. This also applies to the Word of God. We must not only lay up principles that we need but also the Word of God. Instead of running to the Bible whenever you need to hear the Word, hide it in your heart. Matthew 13:52 says, He said to them, "Therefore every teacher of the law who has become a disciple in the kingdom of heaven is like the owner of a house who brings out of his storeroom new treasures as well as old."

2. Helps to Prevent Vain Thoughts

Thoughts hiding the Word of God in our hearts will prevent us from having vain thoughts. In most cases, evil is very present in us mainly because of the level of our spiritual knowledge, which is small. When you have more silver coins in your pocket than gold coins, you will often bring out more silver coins than the gold coin. Having a greater stock of vain thoughts in your heart will make them more available. The same applies to the Word of God in us. When we have more of God's Word, it will exceed all the vain thoughts and become the predominant thought in our hearts. So, it is said in Matthew 12:35, "A good man brings good things out of the good stored up in him, and an evil man brings evil things out of the evil stored up in him."

Our mind will always work on anything it finds in itself the same way a mill grinds anything that we put into it — corn or chaff. You must hide the Word of God in your heart if you want to prevent evil thoughts and avoid musing of vanity on a daily basis.

3. Source of Counsel, Comfort, and Reproof

Sometimes we will be alone without help from other people, and this is when our hearts will provide us with matters of comfort, counsel or reproof. Psalm 16:7 acclaims, "I will praise the Lord, who counsels me; even at night my heart instructs me."

Whenever we are alone and experience a veil of darkness upon the world around us, and we don't have a minister, a Christian friend, a family member to assist us, then our reins will instruct us. At such moments, we would be able to reach out to our hearts for the Word of God, which will refresh us. Every believer needs to be a walking Bible. Have a great knowledge of God's Word in your Heart, and treasure it.

4. Helps us in Prayer

One of the greatest defects that Christians face is the barrenness and leanness of the soul, and many believers complain of it. One of the reasons for that is the lack of God's Word in their hearts. When the heart is often exercised in the Word, God's promises in the Bible will hold or sustain us in prayer and increase our affections to help us pour out our spirits better before Him. Psalm 45:1, "My heart is stirred by a noble theme as I recite my verses for the king; my tongue is the pen of a skillful writer."

When our hearts are full, then our tongue will be free to speak. But have you ever wondered why we find it difficult to open our mouths and pray? One of the reasons is that the heart is barren; when the spring is dry, the stream will not have enough water. Ephesians 6:17-18, "Take the helmet of salvation and the sword of the Spirit, which is the word of God. And pray in the Spirit on all occasions with all kinds of prayers and requests. With this in mind, be alert and always keep on praying for all the Lord's people." But when you have sufficient stock of the Word of God in your heart, it will burst out in prayer.

5. Helps us in our Daily Affairs

God's Word in our hearts will help us in all our affairs as clearly stated in Proverbs 6:21-22, "Bind them always on your heart; fasten them around your neck. When you walk, they will guide you; when you sleep, they will watch over you; when you awake, they will speak to you."

On every occasion, God's Word will be ready to provide us with profitable and godly thoughts. When we wake up each day, the first thoughts in our hearts should begin with God to season our hearts throughout the day. Even as we prepare to engage in our businesses, God's Word will definitely hold our hearts in fear of Him. It will guard us as we sleep at night and prevent us from having vain imaginations and dreams.

The thoughts of the wicked are filled with sinful things. It keeps them busy throughout the day, and at night it also engages them in their dreams and imagination. When the wicked wake up in the morning, sinful thoughts will be the first thing they nurture in their hearts, and the reason is that they are strangers to God's Word. A Christian that is a walking Bible will always be guarded by the Word of God in him to direct him in all his ways and restrain him from sin.

6. A Great Relief in Temptations
Having the Word ready is a great relief in temptations. God's Word is regarded in the Bible as the "Sword of the Spirit." It is the most effective weapon that is available to every Christian during spiritual conflicts. Going about our daily activities without the Word of God leaves Christians vulnerable. We need His Word or the Sword of the Spirit to handle the dangers we may face in life. The more of God's Word in us, the greater our advantage will be when faced with temptations and conflicts.

Our Lord and Savior, Jesus Christ, had the scripture ready when the Devil came to assault Him. He successfully overcame the tempter. When you hide the Word of God in your heart and make use of it pertinently, the door will remain barred upon the Devil, and he won't find an easy entrance. 1 John 2:14, "I write to you, dear children, because you know the Father. I write to you, fathers, because you know him who he is from the beginning. I write to you, young men, because you are strong, and the word of God lives in you, and you have overcome the evil one." We have all it takes to resist the attacks of the Devil when the Word is engrafted in our hearts. We can resist satanic attacks. A believer is prone to sin when she forgets the Word or loses affection for it.

CONCLUSION

The heart is an especially important organ. From a strictly scientific perspective, medical science advises men to be careful about what they allow into their diet because of its damaging impact when it gets to the heart. For example, one is to be wary of food with high cholesterol because they can cause atherosclerosis and lead to heart disease. In this book, the heart has not been looked at in this pure anatomical sense. Instead, it has been viewed from the psychological perspective, in which case it bears a similar meaning to the mind. In this context, our hearts are not affected by just what we eat. They are also affected by what we view, listen to or read. These things influence our thoughts and eventually affect our emotions and, ultimately, our behaviors. We have argued in this book that in order to maintain the sanity of our minds and keep them from being overrun by unclean content, we must make careful decisions about what we view, listen to and read. This decision has to be a daily one. While it is important to avoid certain forms of content, it is also equally helpful to saturate our minds with uplifting content. This is because the battle against unclean hearts is not just about emptying our minds of unclean thoughts but also filling them with noble objectives and pursuits. This is what makes life meaningful and gives man the drive to make daily choices about which content to allow into his mind.

ABOUT THE AUTHOR

The author hails from a rich tropical Caribbean island; Tortola, one of the main lush archipelagos in the British Virgin Islands. Soothing sounds of music or sometimes a blend of folklore inspire her to sway or allow her mind to give way to writing what her mind thinks from the heart in those moments when raw unashamed yet genuine thoughts flow. She enjoys the enchantment of beach scenes and often lays afloat to the undulating melody of the ocean.

Sherron hopes her books touch lives in a phenomenal and vibrating way so much that the words capture each heart into deeper self-love and unconditional love for others. A selfless giver who often wonders why she has a heart impassioned to love and has not met its match with others reciprocating her love as much.

Sherron's vision is to captivate and enthrall hearts to glow beyond their imaginations and that each person recognizes the magnitude of polishing their hearts with frequent positive affirmations. Feel happier as you dance to life's music.

REFERENCES

1. Robinson, M.D & Fetterman, A.K. Do You Use Your Head or Follow Your Heart? Self-Location Predicts Personality, Emotion, Decision Making, and Performance. J Pers Soc Psychol 2013, 105(2): 316–334. doi:10.1037/a0033374

2. Inbar, Y. & Avramova, Y. R. Emotion and Moral Judgment. WIREs Cogn Sci 2013, 4:169–178. doi: 10.1002/wcs.1216

3. Lerner, J. S., Li, Y., Valdesolo, P., & Kassam, K. (014). Emotion and decision making. Annual Review of Psychology.

4. Glynn, J. P. (2012). Emotions: The heart of health. The Criterion.

5. Arnold, J. H. (1997). Freedom from sinful thoughts. The Plough Publishing House, New York.

6. Salem, M. O. (2007). The heart, mind, and spirit.

7. McCrathy, R. (2003). Heart-brain neurodynamics: The making of emotion. Institute of HeartMath, US.

8. Rannamets, H. (2013). How movies influence our dietary behavior. http://www.bfm.ee/about-bfm/bsmr-journal/

9. Zhan, Q., Tian, J. & Xiong, D. (2013). Impact of media violence on aggressive attitude for adolescents. http://dx.doi.org/10.4236/health.2013.512294

10. Chipman, P. R. (2014). Overcoming the Five Primary Negative Thoughts: A Twenty-One Day Mind Renewal Plan for Men. A Thesis Project Submitted to Liberty Baptist Theological Seminary.

11. The Reschini Group. (2007). The heart and mind connection: The link between two vital organs. 12.HeartMath. (2002). The inside story: Understanding the power of feelings. 13. Linden, W. (2014). Healthy behavior is not normal: Exploring the mind-body connection for better health. BC's Mental Health and Addiction Journal Vol. 10, No.2.